Mastering Credit - The Ultimate DIY Credit Repair Guide

Adidas Wilson

Published by Adidas Wilson, 2018.

Copyright © 2020 by Adidas Wilson

All rights reserved. No part of this publication may be reproduced, distributed, or transmitted in any form or by any means, including photocopying, recording, or other electronic or mechanical methods, without the prior written permission of the publisher, except in the case of brief quotations embodied in critical reviews and certain other noncommercial uses permitted by copyright law. For permission requests, write to the publisher, addressed "Attention: Permissions Coordinator," at the address below.

Adidas Wilson
P.O. Box 2262
Antioch, Tn. 37011
siriusvisionstudios@gmail.com
www.adidaswilson.com

While every precaution has been taken in the preparation of this book, the publisher assumes no responsibility for errors or omissions, or for damages resulting from the use of the information contained herein.

MASTERING CREDIT - THE ULTIMATE DIY CREDIT REPAIR GUIDE

First edition. August 25, 2018.

Copyright © 2018 Adidas Wilson.

ISBN: 978-1386926313

Written by Adidas Wilson.

Disclaimer

THE AUTHOR HAS MADE every effort to ensure the accuracy of the information within this book was correct at time of publication. The author does not assume and hereby disclaims any liability to any party for any loss, damage, or disruption caused by errors or omissions, whether such errors or omissions result from accident, negligence, or any other cause.

Table of Contents

Preface
Introduction
Ch. 1 – Credit Reports
Ch. 2 - How to Build Credit
Ch. 3 – Details Matter
Ch. 4 - FICO Credit Score
Ch. 5 - What Is A Good Credit Score?
Ch. 6 - How to Raise Your Credit Scores
Ch. 7 - Equifax, TransUnion, and Experian
Ch. 8 - Consumer Credit Report
Ch. 9 - Free Credit Score or Report
Ch. 10 - How Credit Cards Impact Your Credit Score
Ch. 11 - Mistakes to Avoid When Disputing Credit Report Errors
Ch. 12 - How to Remove A Charge-Off
Ch. 13 - How to Remove Late Payments
Ch. 14 - How to Remove Collections
Ch. 15 - How to Remove A Foreclosure from Your Credit Report
Ch. 16 - How to Remove A Bankruptcy
Ch. 17 - How to Remove A Repossession from Your Credit Report
Ch. 18 - Removing A Judgment
Ch. 19 – How to Remove A Tax Lien from Your Credit Report
Ch. 20 – How to Remove Credit Inquiries from Your Credit Report
Ch. 21 - Sample Credit Dispute Letter
Ch. 22 - Cease and Desist Letter for Debt Collectors
Ch. 23 - Sample Debt Validation Letter
Ch. 24 - How to Deal with Debt Collection Agencies

Ch. 25 - ChexSystems
Ch. 26 - How to Request Debt Validation from Debt Collectors
Ch. 27 - Disputing Credit Card Charges
Ch. 28 - Statute of Limitations on Debt Collection
Ch. 29 - The Fair Debt Collection Practices Act
Ch. 30 - Authorized User
Ch. 31 - Credit Card Piggybacking
Ch. 32 - How to Use Goodwill Letters in Credit Repair
Ch. 33 - Sample Pay for Delete Letter for Credit Report Cleanup
Conclusion
Sample Letters

Preface

Many people assume that credit is a modern invention, probably a couple hundred years old. Obviously, various forms of credit have evolved, and new ones have been invented recently because of technology. Other than that, credit has been in existence long before the official form of money was invented. It is safe to say that credit began with the rising of civilization. People have always borrowed from one another, whether it is money or a cup of sugar. Contrary to popular belief, prostitution is not the oldest profession, the moneylender's job is. With the emergence of civilization, it became clear that a legal system was needed. Some of the earliest recorded laws were about credit and interest. The king of the first Babylon dynasty, Hammurabi, authored the earliest formal law in 1800 B.C and it contains interest regulation laws. It included the maximum interest rate a moneylender could charge. The maximum interest rate for loans of grain was 33 1/3% per annum. The maximum rate for loans of silver was 20% although in some instances it rose as high as 25%. The 20-25% interest rates in Babylon may seem crazily high but they were just as high in India. As per the Laws of Manu in India, the rates were set at 24%. In Babylon, the laws of Hammurabi stated that every loan had to have a public official as a witness and be in a written contract. A moneylender risked severe consequences by charging high interest rates—the debt was cancelled. At the time, collateral was in the form of land or any other possession. It was allowed for a debtor to pledge his slaves, children, or even his wife. If things got bad, some debtors pledged themselves. You could, however, not enslave a debtor for more than three years—the law forbade it. There are records of nations borrowing from other nations as well. Contrary to another misconception, modern banking did not begin after the reformation. Moneylenders may not have accepted deposits on most occasions, but records show that there were two main banking establishments in Babylon that were very similar to the modern-day bank. They accepted deposits, which earned interest and offered loans. One consistent trend of credit and interest throughout history is that a stronger economy translates to a lower interest rate. This, in turn, leads to high levels of confidence and a stronger currency. Nations with low confidence are marked with interest rates that are above world rates. This is evident in developing nations and was the same in ancient nations. The Bronze Age (2400-1200 B.C) was characterized by a vibrant economy across the Aegean Sea. Credit and interest records from this period are vague. The standard value is suspected to have been cattle. Gold was the medium of exchange. This period was followed by events that led to the Dark Age. As the world was recovering from dark times, civilization started flourishing again. Money was coined for the first time during this period by the Lydians, which is (modern-day Turkey). This helped to facilitate international trade. In 594 B.C Athens faced a severe credit crisis and had to make major reforms in the credit laws prescribed by the Laws of Solon. Debts were cancelled, and slavery banned following these reforms. When the Roman Empire gained power, it set new credit regulation laws, with the maximum rate being set at 8 1/3 % per annum. The rates dropped to as low as 4%. When Rome fell, borrowing started being viewed as evil (the Sin of Usury).

Introduction

Frank McNamara founded Diners Club in 1950. He had nothing but big dreams for the establishment and credit cards. He predicted that someday, restaurants would honor the card across New York. His prediction was accurate. Diners Club became the first multipurpose credit card issuer and was accepted widely by merchants. Roughly 72% of consumers in the US carry a credit card. The credit card idea did not start with Diners Club. McNamara's idea just improved something that already existed. In the early 19th century, oil companies and department stores began issuing their customers with "courtesy cards" and metal charge plates for charging purchases. Just like modern-day store cards, the companies that issued them only accepted the cards. Restaurants were not offering these cards then. Diners Club hoped to have its cardboard credit cards accepted widely. Merchants had to pay a 7% fee for every transaction, but they were assured that cardholding customers would spend more than the non-cardholding customers. Cardholders, on the other hand, were promised convenience and a status symbol. The cards had to be paid for in full every month. By the time Diners Club was celebrating its first anniversary, it had attracted a few competitors and 42,000 members. It was the first internationally accepted credit card by 1953. Major companies such as American Express, Bank of America, and Carte Blanche only joined the competition in 1958. Bank of America's credit card proved to be the most innovative. Entertainment, travel outlets, and restaurants only accepted other cards, including Diners Club. The "BankAmericard", despite being limited to California at the time, was accepted by a diverse group of merchants. Bank of America used an unforgettable and rather expensive publicity stunt to introduce its card.

It mailed 60,000 BankAmericards to its customers in Fresno. This was known as the "Fresno drop". This led to widespread fraud, which resulted in the bank losing millions. The card first generated operating profit in 1961. In 1966, the Bank of America started licensing the BankAmericard to banks in different states to boost business. In that same year, Banks in California founded an Interbank Card Association and together managed issuer-merchant transactions. After a while, these organizations became two nationwide networks. They began acting as middlemen between merchants and issuers, confirming the legitimacy of transactions before they went through and completing transactions. BankAmericard became Visa in the long run and broke away from Bank of America. More banks joined ICA and its name changed to MasterCharge and later MasterCard. Sears came up with the Discover card in 1986. It was among the first cash-back cards because it offered consumers a rebate on purchases. The credit card industry continued to grow but even the most fundamental rules remained murky. Lawmakers intervened, and consumer protections were put in place in the 1970s. Discrimination against credit card applicants based on race, sex, or marital status became illegal. Many consumers now use their smartphones instead of plastic cards. They make online purchases using their credit cards without swiping their cards. Some of the information included in your credit report includes whether you have filed for bankruptcy, your criminal record (or lack thereof), your bill payments and home address. This information is sold by credit reporting companies to employers, insurers, and creditors so they can assess your application for employment, insurance, credit, or apartment/home renting. The FCRA (Fair Credit Reporting Act) facilitates the privacy and accuracy of the information. Financial advisors and experts always advise their clients to review their credit reports occasionally. Why is that? The information in these reports affects your eligibility to get loans and the interest you pay. You need to confirm that the information is up-to-date and accurate before applying for a major loan or job. To protect yourself from identity theft. Order your free report. Each of the credit reporting companies, TransUnion, Experian, and Equifax, are required to give you a copy of your report for free, once a year.

The three of them have one website set up, a mailing address and a toll-free number. You can use any one of these channels to order the free annual report.

Website: annualcreditreport.com
Toll-free number: 1-877-322-8228
Mailing address:
Annual Credit Report Request Service
P.O. Box 105281
Atlanta, GA 30348-5281

You can get the report from each of the three or two or just one. But do not contact each one individually. If your credit application is denied based on what is in your credit report, you are entitled to get a free report. But you must put in your request within two months of being notified of the action. In the notice, they include the details of the credit reporting company. You are also eligible for one free report annually if you are on welfare, there's false information in the report due to fraud or you are unemployed and want to find a job within the next two months. The information provider and credit reporting company are responsible for making sure that the information in your report is accurate. Contact the information provider and reporting company to take advantage of your rights. First Step - Write to the reporting company, highlighting the inaccurate information. Support your position with copies of documents. Request them to remove or correct the information. Keep a copy of the letter and documents. The company is required to investigate within 30 days. They then must forward the information you provided to the information provider. The latter will investigate and report the findings back to the reporting company. If changes are made because of the dispute, you will receive a

response in writing and a free credit report. Step Two - Send a dispute letter with supporting documents to the information provider. If they continue to report the disputed item, they are required to inform the credit reporting company about the dispute. And if the information you gave is correct, they are required to let the reporting company know so they can update your report. Some of the information included in your credit report includes whether you have filed for bankruptcy, your criminal record (or lack thereof), your bill payments and home address. This information is sold by credit reporting companies to employers, insurers, and creditors so they can assess your application for employment, insurance, credit, or apartment/home renting. The FCRA (Fair Credit Reporting Act) facilitates the privacy and accuracy of the information. Financial advisors and experts always advise their clients to review their credit reports occasionally. Why is that? The information in these reports affects your eligibility to get loans and the interest you pay. You need to confirm that the information is up-to-date and accurate before applying for a major loan or job. To protect yourself from identity theft. Each of the credit reporting companies, TransUnion, Experian, and Equifax, are required to give you a copy of your report for free, once a year. The three of them have one website set up, a mailing address and a toll-free number. You can use any one of these channels to order the free annual report.
Website: annualcreditreport.com

Toll-free number: 1-877-322-8228

Mailing address:

Annual Credit Report Request Service

P.O. Box 105281

Atlanta, GA 30348-5281

You can get the report from each of the three or two or just one. But do not contact each one individually. If your credit application is denied based on what is in your credit report, you are entitled to get a free report. But you must put in your request within two months of being notified of the action. In the notice, they include the details of the credit reporting company. You are also eligible for one free report annually if you are on welfare, there's false information in the report due to fraud or you are unemployed and want to find a job within the next two months. The information provider and credit reporting company are responsible for making sure that the information in your report is accurate. Contact the information provider and reporting company to take advantage of your rights. Write to the reporting company, highlighting the inaccurate information is the first step. Support your position with copies of documents. Request them to remove or correct the information. Keep a copy of the letter and documents. The company is required to investigate within 30 days. They then must forward the information you provided to the information provider. The latter will investigate and report the findings back to the reporting company.

If changes are made because of the dispute, you will receive a response in writing and a free credit report. Send a dispute letter with supporting documents to the information provider. If they continue to report the disputed item, they are required to inform the credit reporting company about the dispute. And if the information you gave is correct, they are required to let the reporting company know so they can update your report.

Chapter 1
Credit Reports

A credit report is a detailed summary of someone's credit history and is created by credit bureaus. A credit bureau gathers information and prepares credit reports from the information. Lenders analyze and use these reports, together with other important details, to see if a loan applicant is worthy of credit. The United States has three main credit reporting bureaus: Experian, Transunion, and Equifax. Each one of these bureaus collects an individual's bill-paying habits and other personal details to come up with a unique credit report and score. Mostly, the information is similar except for a few small differences among the reports. Credit reports contain personal information including previous and current addresses, employment history, and social security numbers. They also contain credit history summary like the types and number of accounts that are in good standing or past due and detailed account information concerning credit limits, high balances, and date of account opening. The reports outline credit enquiries and information about accounts submitted to credit agencies. In general, credit reports hold negative reports for 7 years and bankruptcy filings stay on a credit report for around 10 years. If someone applies for credit, rental property, or an insurance policy, insurers, creditors, landlords, and a few others are allowed by the law to access their credit report. An employer may also request to have a copy of the report if the person agrees and gives their permission in writing. These parties pay the credit bureaus to attain the report. The credit reporting bureaus are required by the Fair Credit Reporting Act to give customers a free credit report once every year. Consumers can also receive a free credit report when any company takes an unfavorable action against them. The action may include denial of employment, credit, or insurance. Consumers, however, must request for the report within 60 days of the action being taken. Moreover, consumers on welfare, victims of identity theft, and an unemployed person who plans to seek a job within 60 days can also get a free report. The information on credit reports is divided into four sections. At the top are personal details about the individual and in other cases, variances of the Social Security number or person's name because the information was incorrectly reported by a lender or any other involved entity. The second section is a compilation of most reports and has detailed data on lines of credit (trade lines). The third section has public records like tax liens, judgments, and bankruptcies. The bottom section contains a list of all parties that have recently asked to access the person's credit report.

If you see an old address, one you hardly remember, it may cause you to wonder. How are these old addresses acquired by credit bureaus? What Information Is on Your Credit Report? Loan and credit information is not the only thing found on your credit report. It also contains personal information that verifies your identity. You will find all your previous and current addresses, previous and current employers, birthday, and name. Why Would an Old Address Be on a Credit Report? All the addresses where you have received bills before will show up on the credit report—more so loan and credit card statements. When the information is updated by creditors, the address information is also updated. If, for instance, your billing address changes and you inform your credit card issuer, they will report to credit bureaus. Your new address then gets added to your report. The credit bureaus have a record of all your addresses, previous and current. They do not delete old addresses when you relocate. What they do is update the credit report, so it shows what your current address is, based on the reports of your creditors. Fortunately, your address has no effect on your credit score. It does not determine whether creditors accept your applications. Old addresses may be on your report because they do not hurt your score.

Most outdated information falls off your report after a while—but old addresses remain. So, you may find all the addresses where you have received bills or lived on your credit report. What If the Wrong Address Is Listed? Sometimes, your credit report may contain an address that you never lived at or show that you lived somewhere longer than you did. This could be because of identity theft or credit card fraud. Go through your entire credit report slowly and thoroughly, checking for any accounts that do not belong to you. Go an extra mile and assess your credit card statements. See if there are unauthorized charges. Also check the billing address. If there is a case of identity theft, report to the credit bureaus and creditors immediately for the fraudulent accounts to be cleared. It is important to add a fraud alert, so the case never repeats itself in the future. This fraud alert ensures that potential creditors go an extra step to confirm your identity. There is also the option of placing a security freeze—it is free in the U.S. It locks your credit report and prevents new credit inquiries. Additionally, you can have inaccurate addresses removed from your credit report by using a credit report dispute. Note: do not rush to remove your old addresses. Sometimes they are used to confirm your identity. There is no need for you to report your current address to credit bureaus. Lenders and creditors have your current billing address and they report to the bureaus. When someone compromises your personal information, you will be at risk of arrest, denial of credit, unexpected tax bills and identity theft. Over the recent past, data breaches have increased in severity and frequency. Many Americans have experienced the theft of personal information such as Social Security numbers and passport numbers. If, for some reason, you think that you are at risk of identity theft, you may want to consider a credit freeze. A credit freeze or a security freeze prevents businesses from making inquiries on your credit report. Without permission for creditors to access your credit report, it becomes harder for perpetrators to open any fraudulent accounts. Note: even with a credit freeze in place, you will be able to access your own credit score and report. Freezing and unfreezing credit reports is free with the major credit bureaus. All you must do is request for the freeze via phone or online and it will be applied in one business day. If you make the request by mail, it will be done in three business days. You will have a PIN provided by the bureaus or you (depending on the bureau) with which you can lift the freeze. You can also decide to lift the freeze temporarily and specify the duration of the lift. If you want faster results while asking for a temporary lift, you are better off asking over the phone or online. The freeze will be lifted in an hour. If you request the lift by mail, you can expect the lift to be effective in three business days. Note that a freeze will not prevent companies from pulling your report to see if you are right for credit card offers. And do not be surprised if you still receive pre-approved credit offers with a freeze in place. If you like, you can also ask smaller credit bureaus to freeze your report. But you may be charged a fee for freezing and unfreezing. Your other option to protect yourself against identity theft is a fraud alert. But it is weaker than a credit freeze. A fraud alert forces companies to verify your identity using additional steps before they can access your report. With a credit freeze, a company can only check your report once it is lifted. There is another subscription-based service offered by the major credit bureaus. It works like a credit freeze. You lock and unlock your report via a mobile app online. For this service, you must pay a monthly fee—the amount varies by credit bureau. Warning: note that this subscription-based service is not governed by federal law. They can change the terms as they wish. Should You opt for a Credit Freeze? A credit freeze will not guarantee your protection 100%. For instance, a company may decide to give a loan without checking your credit. Additionally, there are other types of crimes such as tax crimes that can be committed using your personal information. So, this is entirely up to you.

Chapter 2
How to Build Credit

It is a little tricky to build credit. Without credit history, you can barely get an apartment, credit card, or loan. Where can you get a history of responsible repayment when you cannot even get credit? To get a FICO score, you need one account (or more) that has been active for at least six months and a creditor reporting your activity to credit bureaus for at least six months. Here are tools to help you build credit history: a credit-builder loan, secured credit cards, authorized user status on someone else's credit card, or a co-signed loan or credit card. Whichever one you decide to use, make sure it gives you a great credit score. A secured credit card is a great idea if you are building your score from the ground up. You pay a deposit amount equal to your credit limit upfront. Utilize the card just as you would any other credit card: use it to make purchases and you have to make a payment before or on the due date, failure to do so would incur late payment fees and interest. If you do not make the payment, your deposit is taken as collateral. When you close your account, you will get your deposit back. You do not have to use a secured credit card forever. It is for building your score so that you become eligible to get an unsecured card. Apply for a credit-builder loan; it is a loan that primarily helps you build credit. It is kind of a forced saving system. When you borrow money, the lender keeps it in an account and only releases it when you have repaid it in full. The lender reports your payments to credit bureaus. Community banks or credit unions usually offer these types of loans. With the use of a co-signer, you can get an unsecured credit card or a loan. Both of you should understand that the co-signer is totally responsible for the full amount owed should you fail to pay. Your significant other or a family member can make you an authorized user on their card. When you are an authorized user, you can access the card and build your credit history. Although you have no legal obligations to pay your share, agree with the cardholder first. They may expect you to pay for your charges or you do not need a card at all from them. Rent-reporting services like RentTrack and Rental Kharma will put a bill you are paying on your credit report. This can show a history of responsible payments. Some credit companies do not consider these payments but there are those that do and that will qualify you to get a credit card or loan, which will, in turn, build your history for all lenders.

Good Habits Will Help You Build Your Score

Make all your payments on time—even utility bills. Maintain low credit utilization. Do not open several new accounts at the same time, as your average account age will be lower. Keep accounts open and active for as long as you can. Always check your annual credit reports for discrepancies and errors. Add primary tradelines such as credit strong, SELF, kikoff.com, MyJewelersClub, Hutton Chase, Fingerhut, Secured Credit Cards. More information found on Financierpro YouTube channel.

Chapter 3
Details Matter

It will help you to know what information is on your credit report and how you should interpret it. Everything that is on your credit profile affects your credit score. Good credit comes in handy when you are looking for financing. Most lenders use the three main credit bureaus, Experian, Equifax, and Transunion to assess your credit history. Credit reports from the three bureaus vary a little but most of the information is the same. The three bureaus have different structures for credit reports with several categories of information considered as neutral, positive, or negative. The information categories include account summary, account history, public records, consumer statement, and credit inquiries. The fastest way to get your credit report is by visiting AnnualCreditReport.com. All of the three bureaus run this site. The law allows you to get your credit report for free once every year (12 months). You are allowed to request all the three reports at the same time, if you like. Some of the information is basic and can be easily interpreted but there are some parts that you need to be familiar with.

Personal Information

This is the easy section but do not skip through it; make sure the information is consistent and accurate. This section contains your name, past and current addresses, social security number, birthday, spouse information, employer and whether it is a joint account. The personal information does not have an impact on your credit score. It is used to confirm your identity. Account Summary contains a summary of your debt history. There are four categories: revolving credit, installment loans, mortgages, and other debts. You will see an outline of the status of debts. In the case of a mortgage you will see the balance, principal loan amount, and the total balances. For revolving credit there is the total balance owed, available credit, credit limit, monthly payment amount, debt to credit ratio, and accounts with a balance. Account History is either very long or short depending on your credit history length. It is a very important section and you should go through it carefully. The account history depicts years of monthly payments you have made on your credit accounts. It is responsible for 35% of your credit score. It is the largest contributor. A credit inquiry is an entry that shows you applied for financing, insurance, or new credit. When you apply for any of these, the company checks your credit, and this affects your score. One or two inquiries may not significantly affect the score, but many inquiries could damage it badly. Lenders may think you are struggling to get credit. Consumer Statement - The information in this section comes from you directly. You can submit a statement when you file a dispute and the credit bureau investigations do not solve anything. Public Records - This section contains bankruptcies, tax aliens, judgments, and any other public records. The information found here impacts your score hugely. The report does not contain your credit score. You will have to buy your score from the credit bureaus.

Chapter 4
FICO Credit Score

The FICO is the credit score used by most lenders to decide whether you qualify for credit. The FICO (Fair Isaac Corporation) model gathers information from the three main credit bureaus and uses this information to calculate three FICO scores for the three bureaus (all three scores are different). Your credit score changes as the information in your credit report changes. The score can change every month or even by day. The algorithm used by Fair Isaac is regularly updated. The newest version is the FICO 9. This new version has several changes such as with the FICO 9 score, paid collections do not negatively affect your credit score. Medical collection accounts have a smaller negative effect on your score. Rental history affects your score if your landlord reports it. This can contribute to good credit history. Apart from the diverse versions of the FICO scoring model, there are various types of the FICO credit score. Each one of them helps lenders determine your financial responsibility. Auto FICO Credit Score: it shows the likelihood of you defaulting on an auto loan or lease. Mortgage FICO Credit Score: it shows the likelihood of you defaulting on a mortgage loan. Credit Card FICO Credit Score: it shows the likelihood of you defaulting on a store charge card or credit card. Installment Loan FICO Credit Score: it shows the likelihood of you defaulting on a large installment loan. Personal Finance FICO Credit Score: it shows the likelihood of you defaulting on a small installment loan. These industry-specific scores are also updated on a regular basis. Fortunately, the calculation of standard FICO scores uses a consistent method across FICO versions. This is how the scores are calculated. Payment history – 35%, Debt owed – 30%, Credit history length – 15%, New credit – 10%, and Credit mix – 10%. Knowing your credit score before approaching a lender may help you know what to expect. Ordering your credit scores is the easiest way to assess them. You must pay for them, either directly through Fair Isaac or through a third-party. If you need a complete outline of the different kinds of scores, deal with Fair Isaac directly. If you decide to deal with a third-party, at least ensure the scores you buy are legitimate. The Vantage Score is a competitor credit scoring model of the FICO Score developed by the three credit bureaus. The two are similar because of the same score range (300-850) but they have some differences such as - Paid collections do not affect your score negatively in the Vantage Score model. Late mortgage payments have a more severe negative impact on your score than any other late payments in the Vantage Score. The Vantage Score will be considerate if you are affected by a natural disaster. The Vantage Score gives you 14 days to rate the shop while the FICO gives you 45 days.

How to Improve A Bad FICO Score

- Minimize your credit card balances.
- Pay your bills on time consistently.
- Remove negative reports on your credit file.

Chapter 5
What Is A Good Credit Score?

Your credit influences every area of your life. A good credit score means lower rates for car loans, credit cards, mortgages, and a few types of insurance. Employers also use credit scores to make hiring and advancement decisions. This chapter will help you understand what a credit score is and what a good or bad score means. Basically, a credit score is a number that shows your likelihood of repaying debts. This number helps creditors decide on whether to give you credit or not and even the terms of the credit. For instance, your bank uses your score to see if you qualify for a mortgage and to decide on the rate; the higher the score the lower the interest rate. Credit bureaus calculate credit scores using their internal algorithms. These scores depend on your financial actions, both present and past. How you pay your debt, amount of debt you owe, and the period you have had credit are some of the factors considered. Your credit score keeps on changing depending on your actions. Simply put, creditors sell your financial information to credit bureaus and the bureaus use the information to come up with your score. This score is like a "grade" of your financial responsibility. New creditors use the credit score to determine your likelihood of repayment. There are many types of credit scores but the one that really counts is the FICO Score. It ranges from 300 to 850.

Others include:

PLUS, Score: it was developed by Experian. It ranges from 330 to 830.

TransRisk Score: TransUnion developed this score and it ranges from 100 to 900.

Equifax Score: it ranges from 280 to 850.

VantageScore: unlike the three models above, lenders use the VantageScore sometimes. It ranges from 300 to 850. The credit you want to obtain and the interest rate that you would prefer are the determining factors on whether your score is good or bad. For a small loan, multiple score ranges are good. Mortgage lenders, however, will require a score of at least 640.

Here are the general range points.

781 and above – excellent credit
661 to 780 – good credit
601 to 660 – fair credit
501 to 600 – poor credit
500 and below – bad credit

Landlords will require that you have a credit score of no less than 620. Otherwise, you will have to get a cosigner. Alternatively, you might be forced to pay a huge deposit.

Average new car rate:

740+ (Super Prime): 2.70%
680 to 739 (Prime): 3.67%
620 to 679 (Non-Prime): 5.49%
550 to 619 (Subprime): 9.25%
<550 (Deep Subprime): 12.42%

Most lenders will not finance you if your score is less than 640. For the best mortgage rates, aim for a score of 720 or higher. For the best rates and a lot of perks, aim for excellent credit (720 and above). A score of 640 and above can also get you a decent credit card.

Chapter 6
How to Raise Your Credit Scores

The behavior of a consumer is prone to change. When a company makes an inquiry, what they get is a "snapshot" of your situation. When you open a charge account, miss a payment, or pay your debt, your score changes. Although the number keeps changing, you need to know what your score is at a time and how you can increase it. Each section of credit information carries a different weight when it comes to calculating your credit score. 35% payment history - This is very important as it contributes the largest share. Underpayments, missed payments, late payments, and other related issues are included in this section. Creditors report this kind of information differently (some 10 days after the due date, some after you have missed two payments, etc.). Get to know how your creditor reports information. 30% outstanding debt - You have a credit limit and you are the determinant of that limit. Your outstanding debt is calculated against unused credit and used to come up with a credit score. Many credit cards increase your credit limit (if you do not use up the available credit). 15% length of credit history -Keeping your account for a long period of time boosts your credit score. The most important thing is to pay off your balances and avoid closing accounts. If you use the same finance resource for different loans you will also help your score. 10% new credit information - New credit shows that you can open credit lines and that your financial situation is great since creditors are willing to finance you. It also shows that you are financially active. 10% credit mix - A mortgage is a loan; so is a credit card and any other account that you can charge groceries or gas to. However, they are not the same type of loans. Their difference is important. Several kinds of credit accounts show credit bureaus that you can handle different types of financing. Negative items such as tax aliens, judgments, and bankruptcies can damage your score. Credit bureaus accumulate all the factors above and use their formula to come up with a number that is your score. The number changes regularly and you should check your credit report on a regular basis. You can improve a bad credit score by adopting good credit habits, not over-borrowing, paying on time, and keeping low credit balances. Dispute negative items on your report; you can do it yourself or involve a credit repair company. Credit repair involves challenging and verifying inaccurate information. It works to retain the good information and eliminate bad information.

Chapter 7
Equifax, TransUnion, and Experian

Your credit report contains information from each of these bureaus and it affects your access to credit. It is a determining factor on whether you get a credit card, when you apply, and the interest rate you will be charged among other things. But why are there three of them? How are they different? Surprisingly, the three credit bureaus are not affiliated with the government. They are private institutions that get information from creditors about your financial behavior and history. Contributors of this information include credit card companies, banks, cell phone companies, healthcare providers, utility companies, and lenders. Each of these bureaus evaluates your credit report and sells the information to lenders whenever you apply for a credit card or loan, with your permission. Sometimes, potential employers and landlords will require this information as well. The information determines your creditworthiness. A while back, whenever you asked the local bank for a loan they would ask around to see how much you owe and whether you pay your debts on time. However, the population increased rapidly, and people barely stayed in the same place for long, so bigger financial institutions had to be formed. With this advancement, banks had a difficult time tracking everyone's financial history. With time, financial groups and retailers started making lists of customers with bad and good credit. Failure to pay your bills landed you on the blacklist and the lists were sold to creditors to assess loan applicants. Eventually, these led to the rise of three different companies: Equifax, TransUnion, and Experian. These are the three main ones but there are many more credit reporting companies. Most of them, however, only collect certain types of financial information. Each of them is a separate company, operated differently from the rest and provides a different level of detail on certain kinds of information. For instance, Experian and Equifax will only record your employer's name under your employment history while TransUnion records more details such as the employment period and your title. When you get your credit report from the three bureaus, you will notice the difference. When information is missing on either one of the reports, you have no reason to be concerned, but you should be if there is inaccurate information. The credit scores vary because the information on each report is slightly different. Another thing, the scoring methods are not the same. Experian uses the FICO 8 Score. It is what you will see when you buy your credit score from them. Creditors and lenders may ask for different FICO versions or the VantageScore. TransUnion provides creditors and lenders with both the VantageScore and FICO. Equifax provides creditors with both the VantageScore and FICO but if you buy your score from the site it uses the Equifax Credit Score Model.

For mailing purposes:

TransUnion P.O. Box 1000 Chester, PA 19022   1-800-916-8800

Equifax   P.O. Box 740241 Atlanta, GA 30374-0241 1-800-685-1111

Experian   P.O. Box 2104 Allen, TX 75013-0949   1-888-397-3742

Chapter 8
Consumer Credit Report

A great credit rating can affect your finances in several ways, so it is important for you to learn how to interpret your consumer credit report. When you apply for credit cards, lines of credit, or loans, lenders consider your credit score. This score partially determines your approval for new credit and even the interest rate to be applied on what you are borrowing. Credit scores are not a product of guesswork. The data in your credit report is used to calculate them. Fair Isaac Corporation is the original developer of the FICO score. 90% of lending decisions are made based on the FICO score. It ranges from 300 to 850 (850 being the perfect score). Another credit-scoring model that is giving FICO a run for its money is the VantageScore. Its numeric range is the same as that of the FICO. More than 2,400 lenders used the model from July 2015 to June 2016—and this includes 20 of the 25 topmost financial institutions. The average VantageScore was 673 and the average FICO score was 700 as of 2017. The VantageScore and the FICO models do not use the same algorithms to come up with credit scores but they both depend on information from consumer reporting agencies. Knowing how to read your credit report will set you on the path towards a better credit health. A credit report can look like many confusing numbers at first glance. However, if you learn what is on it you will be able to decipher it easily. Credit reports are usually made up of five main parts. Personal Information: your credit history and your Social Security number are linked. So, the SS number, together with your name, birthday, and current address will be on the credit report. Included would also be your employment history, previous addresses, and any other names. Credit Accounts: most probably, this will be the biggest section of your report. It contains all your past and current credit accounts such as type of account, current balance, creditor's name, date of account opening and closing, payment history, and total credit limit. Collection Items: when you fail to pay your debt, your creditor might transfer it to a collection agency, and it will appear on your credit report. This can really damage your score. Public Records: a debt collector can sue you for failing to pay a debt. If he wins, the court enters a judgment against you which may show up on your report. Inquiries: the lender will most likely check your credit score and report when you are applying for new credit. This is known as hard inquiry. Every new credit inquiry goes to your credit report. Your Credit Report and Credit Scoring

The following factors affect your FICO scores:

- Payment history
- Credit utilization
- Length of credit history
- Credit mix
- New credit

Payment history carries more weight than the others. The VantageScore model is affected by the following:

- Payment history
- Age and type of credit
- Percentage of credit limit used
- Total balances/debt
- Recent credit behavior and inquiries
- Available credit

Knowing all these will help you adopt habits that could build your score, for instance, paying off some of your debt. Also, learn to review your credit report on a regular basis to check for errors or attempts of identity theft.

Chapter 9
Free Credit Score or Report

Have you reviewed your credit report lately? You probably have not checked it for some time now. According to a 2014 Financial Literacy Survey by National Foundation for Credit Counseling, 65% of American citizens had not asked for their credit report in a year, even though they can get a free annual copy from Annualcreditreport.com. That is not wise because errors on your credit report that go undetected could cost you points and lead to loan denials or very high interest rates should you be approved for a loan or credit card. There are several ways through which a consumer can check their credit report or various versions of the credit score for free. The first step, however, is knowing what is on the report. A credit report has different objectives from a credit score, according to Gail Cunningham, a National Foundation for Credit Counseling spokesperson. She says that a credit report is a record of your past and present financial activity. It offers a summary of who you are financially. The information in a credit report includes your past and present residence, bill payment history, financial judgments against you, monthly payment and balance of your credit accounts, and the age of the accounts. A credit score, on the other hand, is a numerical representation of your credit report information. Lenders use it to evaluate risk and it strongly determines whether you will be extended credit. Your credit score ranges from 300 to 850. It was developed by Fair Isaac Corporation (FICO) and is used to determine whether you will pay your bills on time. You have two credit scores: a FICO educational score (consumer score) and a FICO score. Lenders and creditors use the FICO score while the consumer score is the one that consumers can get in several ways. The Fair and Accurate Credit Transactions Act requires that all Americans be given free access to their credit reports from the three bureaus (TransUnion, Equifax, and Experian) once every year. AnnualCreditReport.com is the easiest site from which to get these reports. You also get access to a free report if you are denied credit, are a victim of identity theft or fraud, or your current credit has changed. The law does not require any institution to give you free access to your credit score and you cannot get it from AnnualCreditReport.com free of charge. You can buy your FICO score but there are ways to view your score for free. A score report costs $19.95 on MyFICO.com. You can also buy the consumer version from any of the credit bureaus (the number could be higher than your FICO score). The lending process can be confusing because the digit that the lender uses may be different from what you see. It is, therefore, advisable to buy the FICO score.

These are the best sites to view your FICO consumer version score:

- Creditkarma.com
- CreditSesame.com
- Credit.com
- Quizzle.com

You can check as many times as you want. The numbers are usually higher than the actual FICO score that lenders and banks will see. Although the consumer credit scores vary from FICO scores, you can assess your credit health or catch fraud attempts by reviewing them.

Chapter 10
How Credit Cards Impact Your Credit Score

Credits cards are a double-edged sword when it comes to attaining a high credit score. The way you use your cards will determine whether your score increases dramatically or drops drastically. Credit cards carry the most weight than any other type of debt as far as credit scores are concerned because they clearly show how you borrow and manage your debts. You choose how much to charge and pay each month— this free will is not offered with other kinds of debt. Although each credit scoring system uses a unique model, the following credit card habits can impact your credit score negatively or positively. Generally, having a credit card will help your credit score. The credit scoring systems need to see how you handle different kinds of debt. This helps them find a mix of revolving debt and installment debt. Your credit mix makes up 10% of the FICO score. If you do not own a credit card, you can still prove that you are responsible and boost your credit score if you have other loans like car notes and mortgages. However, if you desire to have a very high credit score (close to the perfect 850 score), you will need a good reward card that is within your means then make use of it responsibly. Anytime you apply for credit, the card issuer will run a credit check. A higher credit score means that you are likely to pay your bills responsibly and so your new card will have a lower interest rate. Many credit inquiries in a short time will drop your credit score because according to research, someone looking for credit has higher chances of falling into financial problems than someone who is not. Creating new credit accounts can cause your credit score to drop temporarily but a difference could come if you try making a huge purchase (like a house or a car) in the same period. On the other hand, creating new credit accounts might have a negative effect. One of the factors that affect your score is your debt amount relative to your credit amount; this is known as the credit utilization ratio). The lower the credit utilization rate the better. After paying off your credit card debt, you will probably choose to close the credit card accounts that you do not use anymore. However, that may hurt your credit. It may increase your credit utilization ratio because then, your available credit will be less. Put the card away instead, or just cut it if you do not trust yourself. Credit cards are amazing, but they can seriously harm your score if you overuse the credit available to you. Your debt makes up 30% of your FICO score. It hugely influences VantageScore as well. Either pay all the credit balances each month or keep the balances very low. Paying your bills late is a very damaging habit. Payment history accounts for 35% of the FICO score and greatly influences your VantageScore. Multiple credit cards might increase your credit score which in turn leads to benefits like access to loans, among others. Multiple credit cards can also be risky. All your credit accounts (student loans, mortgages, auto loans, store revolving accounts, and credit cards) account to 10% of your score. Whether you have one or ten credit cards, what really matters is how you use the card and whether you pay your bills before they are due. On average, Americans own three to four credit cards. There exists a correlation between more credit cards (seven) and a higher credit score (800+) according to Credit Karma. According to Mint's credit reporting tool, "0-5 credit accounts is poor, 6-12 is not bad, 13-21 is good, and 22 or more (open or closed) is excellent". This is for all credit types and it accounts for just a small part of your credit score. Multiple cards might have a negative effect, but your credit score will not depreciate because you own several cards. Just make sure you are not opening and closing so many cards at the same time. The number of credit cards impacts some of the most crucial factors are total debt owed in relation to your credit limit. A new credit card increases the total credit limit. Alternatively, you can ask your credit issuer to raise your limit instead of getting a new one. This is better than getting a new card because you will have only one card to manage and you will avoid the negative effect of a credit inquiry. However, one inquiry takes less than five points so if your credit score is excellent and credit history is long, new accounts may not have much of an impact. Another factor is the percentage of debt carried on each credit card. So that is why you should have no less than three credit cards. If you spend more than 20% of your limit per month, spreading the balance will help your credit score. People get credit cards for convenience as well as the rewards. Chasing the rewards, however, may not be worth it. You can use one card that offers travel points and another one that offers high cash back for groceries and gas. Different types of cards have diverse reward programs. Here are the disadvantages to having multiple credit cards. Opening too many new credit cards will impact your credit history and consequently, your score. Some cards are not easy to maintain. With more cards and a high credit limit, you may spend too much.

Chapter 11
Mistakes to Avoid When Disputing Credit Report Errors

You can easily undermine your ability to challenge a case and even undermine your own consumer rights when disputing errors on your credit report. The Fair Credit Reporting Act requires credit reporting agencies (Equifax, Experian, and TransUnion) to investigate any dispute raised by you concerning your credit report. The same applies to the institutions that provide the credit bureaus with your financial information. In case they do not review your case seriously and the errors remain, you have the right to sue them. However, your case will only succeed if you take the time to prepare. If a lender misreports your information to a bureau, do not go around the credit reporting agency and deal with the lender. If the lender does not correct the mistake, you cannot fight back. Sending your dispute to the credit bureau first triggers a serious investigation as required by the FCRA. You cannot sue the lender or furnisher for not investigating your dispute if you did not send it to the credit reporting agency first. Another thing, your issue has a chance of being solved faster if you send the dispute to the credit bureau as opposed to the furnisher. If you have sent several disputes to a credit reporting agency and they did not resolve it, the best thing is to sue the credit bureau. Nevertheless, if you do not have the necessary evidence or documents to prove the mistake, your case may not be solid. The case is usually stronger if you have filed several disputes on your own to no availability and you can prove the harm that has been done to you. It is difficult to convince a jury without sufficient evidence and your case will be moved to summary judgment.

Be sure to save all important documents, including the certified mail receipt that proves the bureau received the dispute. People often prefer the most convenient option and file their dispute by phone or online. Credit reporting agencies seem to encourage this by convincing consumers about their easy to use online dispute systems. This might cost you a lot if you decide to sue the credit bureau. Remember while filing that dispute online you will be using a form provided by the bureau and you will, most probably, not attach sufficient information or evidence. Do not file your disputes online, instead, send the credit bureau a detailed letter and include sufficient evidence. Most people never bother to read the terms (usually found at the bottom of a web page) when they accept a free report or purchase one from a credit bureau. For instance, the terms of TransUnion contain an arbitration clause. This might prevent your right to argue the case in front of a jury. Now you see why it is better to file a dispute by mail. Alternatively, read the terms carefully and make sure you understand. Negative information should be cleared from your credit report after seven years according to the law (or ten years in the case of bankruptcy). It is your right to dispute a debt on your report if it is older than seven years. A debt collector cannot sue you for a debt that is expired. A problem arises, however, if you re-age a debt accidently while conversing with a debt collector. Avoid talking to a debt collector and never agree to pay an expired debt.

Chapter 12
How to Remove A Charge-Off

A charge-off occurs because of serious defaulting on an account, that is, you are late by 180 days or more. Your creditor will list the account as "not collectible" when a charge-off occurs. Lenders will list a debt as a charge-off mainly for tax reasons; so, the item can be considered a loss. However, they will still expect you to pay the debt. Even with a charge-off on your credit report, creditors will not stop trying to collect the debt. Charge-offs remain on your report for seven years. They can greatly impact your score. A charge-off on your credit report is one of the worst items you can have and even one can cause your loan applications to be declined. However, there is a way to remove it from your report before the seven years is up. Paying a charge-off is better than not paying it at all and may impact your score slightly. Nevertheless, it is still a negative item even when you pay it and will influence your score until it expires. The impact lessens with time, but potential lenders will see it. Therefore, your chances at low interest rates and credit approval might still get hurt. When to Pay A Charge-Off? The charge-off is recent: a new charge-off can really reduce your score. The higher your credit score, the more points it will deduct. If you can, pay the charge-off and ask your creditors to remove it from your report. You must pay it to qualify for a home loan: in most cases in the mortgage industry, you will be required to clear off all your debt before you can get a loan. Talk to the lender to see how you can settle the debt. Pay it if the creditor will re-age/delete it: if you clear the debt totally, some creditors will have no problem removing it from your file. Others might agree to re-age the debt. When Not to Pay A

Charge-Off? The charge-off is listed with different companies: if a charge-off is listed with multiple collection agencies, make sure you verify the current owner of the debt before paying it off. You are not sure the amount listed is what you owe: debt collectors may add phony interest and fees. If you did not sign an agreement with the original creditor to allow third-party agencies to add their own interest and fees, they cannot do this. A debt that you paid off can also erroneously end up as a charge-off on your report. It is past the statute of limitations: nonpayment of a debt cannot be brought against you if it is past the statute of limitations. Can A Charge Off Be Deleted from Your Credit Report? One way to have a charge off removed is by agreeing on a "pay for delete" arrangement with your creditor. Try carrying out the negotiation in writing. Secondly, you can file a dispute with the credit bureaus. If the charge-off account cannot be verified, they are required to remove it from your report.

Chapter 13
How to Remove Late Payments

Your credit score will suffer if your credit report has records of late payments. Your payment history greatly affects your score. There are a few ways to get late payments removed from your report; but first, check out the effects of late payments on your score. A single late payment on your credit report can have a huge negative impact. A late credit card payment, car payment, mortgage payment, or any other late payment can decrease your FICO score by 90 to 110 points. With time, the effect of the late payment lessens until it expires. Nevertheless, if the negative account is on your report, creditors will still be able to see it. The late payments appear as 30, 60, 90, or 120+ days late. The various degrees of delinquency affect your score differently, the later the payment, the bigger the damage. Recent late payments affect your score more than older ones. A creditor reports a late payment when it is 30 days overdue. Some creditors may choose not to report at all while others will report when you close your account. If the payment is late by 90 days or more, your credit score will suffer more. It may even be reported as a charge-off if your lender sells the outstanding debt to a collection agency. The amount you owe does not matter, a late payment of $60 has the same effect as a late payment of $6000. A late payment will stay on your report for seven years. Fortunately, this does not mean that you must wait seven years to establish credit. Your credit score will begin to rise again steadily, and you can even get a late payment permanently removed from your report. You can get a late payment updated to "never late" or removed completely. There are a few simple ways to do this. The approach you decide to go with depends on the relationship you have with your creditor, your credit history, and the amount of effort you are willing to put into the process. You have options. Requesting A Goodwill Adjustment is ideal if your relationship with your creditor is good. Requesting a goodwill adjustment means asking the lender to remove the late payment as a goodwill gesture since you have been a great client. Write a letter to the creditor explaining why you are late and why you need the late payment removed. Signing up for automatic payments may prompt the creditor to agree to remove the late payment. Both of you win here in that, the creditor is assured of timely payment and your credit report will be one less negative account. Check the late payment information for any inaccuracies. Then file a dispute by sending a hard copy letter to the credit bureaus. They are required by law to carry out an investigation. Seek the help of a professional credit repair company. There are good credit repair companies. This is a great option if you have no time or you have some money to spare.

Chapter 14
How to Remove Collections

Collections on your credit report do not help your credit score. Removing collections from your report is no easy task, but it is doable. First, learn how collections impact your credit and how to remove them. Collections, like most negative accounts, stay on your report for a maximum of seven years. Paying it will not have it removed; it will only be updated to "paid collection". A collection is filed differently from a charge-off account from your original creditor. An account will most likely end up in collections if it is 4 to 6+ months overdue. At this point, your creditor no longer contacts you about the loan. It is never a nice feeling having your debt turned over to a collection agency. When collections are first recorded on your credit report, your score will drop 50 to 100 points, the higher your credit, the more the points. The effect of a collection account reduces with time. The original creditor notifies you before they send the account to collections. The most common accounts include cable/satellite and local utility services like Direct TV, Comcast, Time Warner, Dish, and Cox. Medical debt and some credit card accounts are also commonly sent to collections. FICO's new version ignores paid collection accounts. In this new version also, medical collections affect your score less. VantageScore's new algorithm does not consider paid collections. These updates mean that paying off your collection accounts will help your credit. However, financial institutions are still in the process of adopting the new scoring models. It may, therefore, take a while for you to see a positive impact. Before you pay off a debt, make sure you owe it first. Send a validation request to the agency. They must prove their ownership of the debt, otherwise, they cannot act regarding the debt. The Fair Credit Reporting Act (FCRA) sets the reporting limit and it is currently set at seven years after the last activity date. The statute of limitations, on the other hand, is different in various states. It ranges from three to six years or more. The removal of collections can greatly impact your credit score in a positive way. It is common to find inaccuracies in collection accounts because information is easily omitted or misreported as the debt is passed from one agency to another. The law allows you to dispute any inaccurate information on your credit report or even any accounts that you are not sure about. You can choose to file the dispute on your own or better, involve a professional. Professionals are good at this and you will have greater chances of success.

Chapter 15
How to Remove A Foreclosure from Your Credit Report

Dealing with a foreclosure is never easy. In addition to losing your home, you face the consequences of low credit scores brought on by foreclosure. This gives you a very difficult time as you try to get back on your feet. A foreclosure can be removed from your report. Lenders make mistakes and there are times when banks must pay restitution due to mismanaged foreclosures. It is not uncommon to find errors in foreclosure cases. Therefore, having a foreclosure permanently removed is possible. A foreclosure can also be removed due to lack of available records. This happens when the owner of the mortgage goes out of business. Even if the mortgage is sold to another bank, there is a possibility of errors occurring during the process. If this happens and the new owner cannot verify your foreclosure, it must be removed from your credit report. After you get copies of your credit report from the three bureaus, go through the foreclosure entries very carefully. If there is any inaccurate information, you can file a dispute. Do not make the common mistake of assuming that all the three credit reports are the same. The credit bureaus have different methods of filing this kind of information. If the credit bureaus refuse to remove the foreclosure, ask the lender to remove it, citing the inaccuracies. Give them a deadline (30 days). If they cannot verify the information, they might remove it. You must file three different disputes with the three credit bureaus. How you word each of these disputes is extremely important; otherwise, they will deem it "frivolous". Your communication and the proof you provide will affect the bureaus' decision to act on your dispute. Therefore, it is important to get professional help. When a foreclosure first appears on your report, expect your score to drop 80-160 points, the better the score, the sharper the drop. You may notice an increase in the interest rates on your credit cards as well. You also might not qualify for new credit. Years ago, it was possible to negate the damage of a foreclosure by completing a deed-in-lieu or a short sale. However, now the implications are the same (although you can qualify for a mortgage after a short sale). It will take you two years or more to qualify for a mortgage. When you do, you will have to pay a higher down payment and higher interest rates. A foreclosure will remain on your report for seven years, but its effect lessens with time. The same applies to a short sale. How Does A Foreclosure Affect Your Life? The credit score is used: By employers in the hiring process. In setting insurance rates. In determining approval for utilities. In other services such as internet and cable. By landlords to screen potential renters

Chapter 16
How to Remove A Bankruptcy

Dealing with bankruptcy is tough, but you are not alone. Bankruptcy comes with consequences, as far as your credit is concerned, and even after it has been discharged, you will have some work to do. How do you repair your credit after bankruptcy? What do you need to know? The length of time depends on the type of bankruptcy. A Chapter 13 bankruptcy will be on your report for 7 years while a Chapter 7 bankruptcy will be on your report for 10 years. However, there is a way to get a bankruptcy removed from your credit report before the 7 or 10 years and you can still get credit. Waiting a few years to get credit may be too much for some people, especially because even after you qualify for credit you will have to pay crazy interest rates. Instead of waiting too long and paying ridiculous rates, work to reduce the negative effects of your bankruptcy. You will be able to repair your credit and receive great credit offers. A bankruptcy on your credit report can damage your credit score in a huge way. It will take 130-150 points from your FICO if you have a score of 680 and 220-240 points if your credit score is 780. This drop will, most likely, cause creditors to decline your credit applications and if you qualify, they will charge high interest rates. Moreover, the amount you can borrow will be limited. Even when filing for bankruptcy is your best option, you need to be aware of the implications. The first and most important step would be to remove the bankruptcy from your credit report. Another important thing is assessing and changing your financial habits, so you never have to file for bankruptcy again. Check your income and expenses and put something into your emergency fund. One habit you really need to cultivate is the habit of paying your bills on time. Your payment history is the biggest determinant of your credit score. As you strive to repair your credit, do not accrue new debt. At least, filing for bankruptcy gets most of your debt discharged. Credit bureaus will have you thinking it is not possible; but you can get a bankruptcy removed. If you file a dispute concerning your bankruptcy, file three different disputes with all three bureaus. They are separate companies and you cannot file one and expect it to apply to them all. In your dispute, state the facts and do not be guided by your emotions. It is totally possible to do this on your own. However, the process can be tedious and lengthy and positive results are not guaranteed. You dispute the bankruptcy by asking the bureaus how they verified your bankruptcy or by pointing out inaccurate information in your credit report. The bureaus are required by law to respond within 30 days. If they do not verify it, they will send you a written statement and you can use it to have the bankruptcy removed. Before you dispute, suppress your profile with LexisNexis. After you suppress your file, freeze your file with LexisNexis as well other third-party companies that collect consumer information. Now you want to obtain a document from the local bankruptcy clerk saying they do not report to third parties. This can also be found on their website. All files must have a credit freeze prior to sending a 609 Dispute Letter to the three major credit agencies Equifax, Experian, Transunion. You can also include public record removal letters.

Innovis Security Freeze Options
1-800-540-2505
https://www.innovis.com/securityFreeze/index
Advance Resolution Services A.R.S.)
1-800-392-8911 (no website)
Sagestream (formely ID Analytics)
1-888-395-0277
https://www.sagestreamllc.com/security-freeze/

LexisNexis
1-888-497-9172
https://www.lexisnexis.com/privacy/
Corelogic/CREDO
1-877-532-8778
http://www.corelogic.com/solutions/credco-consumer-assistance.aspx (information only)
Factor Trust
1-844-773-3321
https://ws.factortrust.com/consumer-inquiry/request-your-credit-report/
Clarity Services Inc.
1-866-390-3118
https://www.clarityservices.com/support/security-freeze/
Microbilt
1-800-884-4747 option #5
1-888-222-7621
http://www.microbilt.com/us/consumer-affairs
(Freeze all third-party companies prior to disputing a bankruptcy)

Below is an example of what you should receive from the bankruptcy courts before disputing with the three major credit bureaus. Also, read below to send an email to Pacer. Make sure you email them for your records. Below is what they sent me. Hi, my name is (place your name) and i wanted to know the procedure or the process you use when validating and reporting public records to credit bureaus. Thank you.

Public Access to Court Electronic Records (PACER) is an electronic public access service of the United States Federal Courts that allows users to obtain case and docket information from Federal Appellate, District and Bankruptcy courts through the Internet. PACER does not contact consumer reporting and credit reporting agencies. PACER simply provides access to federal court records.

Thank you,
PACER Service Center
Phone: 210-301-6440
Toll Free: 800-676-6856
For Frequently Asked Questions: http://www.pacer.gov/psc/hfaq.html
For Account Information: https://www.pacer.gov/psco/cgi-bin/psclogin.pl

Below is an example to include with the 609-dispute letter. This is after you place a security freeze with third party companies.

Consumer Credit Reports Information

All bankruptcy case filings appear for 7-10 years from the date the case was filed on a credit report. Federal Law 15 U.S.C. §1681c, "Requirements relating to information contained in consumer reports," provides information regarding bankruptcy cases and what can be disclosed. Bankruptcy records are public records unless sealed, and all information contained in them can be retrieved by anyone, including credit reporting agencies. The U.S. Bankruptcy Court is not responsible for credit reports. Any disputes with a credit agency must be resolved by the debtor and that agency. If you wish to obtain a copy of documents filed in your case, you may set up an account with www.pacer.gov, or you may come to our office at 701 Broadway, Nashville, TN 37203. If you come to our office, the price for copies varies. If you print the documents, it is $0.10 per page. If the Clerk prints the documents, it is $0.50 per page. The Clerk accepts cash, cashier's check, or money order. Cashier's checks and money orders must be made payable to U.S. Bankruptcy Court. Filing for bankruptcy is never anyone is first option. However, sometimes it is the best thing you can do to help your financial situation. It is a negative account on your credit report, but it frees you from debt. Here is all you need to know about bankruptcy. Bankruptcy is basically the process of eliminating debt or satisfying it under different terms. It is a serious decision but if you cannot pay back everything you owe, it can set you free from debt. The two major types of bankruptcy are Chapter 7 and Chapter 13. The other one is Chapter 11— it is usually for businesses but can also apply to individuals. Chapter 7 bankruptcy is for people who meet specific income guidelines and cannot afford to satisfy the debt using a repayment plan. There is a means test that you must pass to qualify. It is the fastest and cheapest option. With this type of bankruptcy, your personal property is likely to be sold off to satisfy the debt instead of you making payments. If you want to protect some belongings from being sold off, you need to apply for exemptions. This depends on the debt you owe. You can use a Chapter 7 delinquency to delay a foreclosure process. As for unsecured debts like personal loans or credit cards, you may be able to file for an exemption on your car, home, or other major items to protect them from being auctioned or repossessed. Your state laws will determine the eligible exemptions. Chapter 13 bankruptcy is for people who make a lot of money, preventing them from qualifying for a Chapter 7. Its advantage is that your property will not be sold off, but you will have to pay your lenders over the next three to five years. The repayment plan varies. All secured debts, priority debts, and administrative fees must be repaid in full for you to keep your property. Your income determines the duration of the plan and the amount you will pay on unsecured debt. Chapter 11 is mostly for companies, but individuals may apply. You can qualify if your debt level surpasses the limits of Chapter 13. Chapter 11 is like Chapter 13 in most ways such as security of property from repossession. The main difference is that you must repay your debt over a five-year period. There is no option to reduce the period. A bankruptcy is bad for your credit score. It can deduct 160 to 220 points from the score. A Chapter 13 bankruptcy remains on your report for seven years. A Chapter 7 can stay for ten. The effects, however, lessen with time. Getting credit immediately after a bankruptcy will be a challenge; but with time, you will begin to qualify. You may still have to pay crazy interest rates. A mortgage will be the hardest to get. Is Bankruptcy the Best Option for You? There is no simple answer to this question and the decision lies with you. Talk to a credit counselor so they can walk you through it. Most importantly, figure out how you got here and how you can avoid such a pitfall next time. Even though a bankruptcy will linger on your report for a while, there are useful tips to help you improve your score and become eligible for credit, even with the bankruptcy still on your file. This is no easy task, but it is possible. Talking to a professional will provide knowledge and experience and could get the account permanently deleted from your report before the seven years. In the process, they can get other negative items removed from your report as well. Some people get into financial troubles due to situations that are out of their control such as medical emergencies or a job loss. Other people get into trouble because of careless spending. Whatever the reason for filing for bankruptcy, try your best to make sure it never happens again. If you have a problem with overspending, come up with a monthly budget and stick to it. If an emergency is the reason for your financial hardship, consider setting aside a rainy-day fund. Even if money is tight, find ways to help you spend less so you can save. A credit card is a quick and effective way to improve your credit. You may be hesitant because more debt is not exactly what you are looking for, but a positive payment history affects your score more than any other component. Instead of charging all your expenses to your card, pick a single bill to pay with your credit card every month and then repay the balance immediately. A long history of on-time payments will start to increase your score. How do you get a credit card with a bankruptcy? You have the option of both secured and unsecured credit cards (even immediately after a bankruptcy). A secured credit card requires you to place a refundable deposit equal to your credit limit. The deposit is security and you will be paying for the card balance out of your own pocket. Ensure that the credit card issuer reports your monthly activities to the three credit bureaus. Do not apply for multiple credit card applications as this could hurt your score even more. Before you start thinking about a car, be responsible with your credit card for at least six months. This shows that you can repay your debts and improves your score. Also, set aside some money to use as a down payment, even if you are eligible for the full amount. Remember you will, most likely, must pay a higher interest rate. Consider a used car rather than a brand new one. Buying a house will have to wait for a while depending on the type of bankruptcy you filed for and the loan you want. You will have to get permission from the court and have a 12-month history of on-time payments. You might also have to pay a higher down payment and interest. Because of this, spend the seasoning period making responsible financial decisions and rebuilding your credit.

Chapter 17
How to Remove A Repossession from Your Credit Report

A repossession on your credit report will damage your credit score. It may cause you to be denied a car loan, home loan, and even credit card offers. A car repossession will be on your credit report for seven years. Its effect reduces with time but if it is there, it will affect your score negatively. Repossession occurs when you default an auto loan. You are usually required to make monthly payments. Until you pay the loan in full, the bank that gave you the loan owns the car. If you fail to make the payments, the bank has a right to take back the car. The creditor can take the car anytime as long as you have defaulted on the loan. In some states, the law does not require them to notify you before they repossess the car. They take it and try to resell it to get back their money. It does not make any difference whether you voluntarily surrender the car, or they take it. The implications on your credit score are the same. Even after repossessing the vehicle, the bank can decide to sue you for the remaining amount. For instance, assume you owe $15000 for a car and it gets repossessed. If the creditor sells it for $10000, they might sue you for the additional $5000. If they sue you, there will be a judgment on your credit report—which makes things even worse for you. You do not have to wait seven years to have a repo removed from your credit report. There are two things that you can do. First, you can get the bank to agree to a renegotiation of payment terms. If they accept the new terms, they can remove the repo from your report. If they agree to remove it, make sure the agreement is in writing. Second, you can dispute the repossession account. If the creditor fails to verify your repossession or does not reply to your dispute within 30 days, you can get it dropped from your report. If you doubt your ability to file and follow through with a dispute, seek help from a professional credit repair company. It is possible to get a car loan if you have the repossession removed from your credit report. It will be difficult to get financing for a car with the repossession still on your report. If a creditor agrees to finance you, they will charge you very high interest rates and you end up paying way more than the car is worth.

Chapter 18
Removing A Judgment

Judgments can harm your credit score in a huge way, making it hard for you to obtain credit. Your judgment could be a result of a lawsuit from a former eviction or old debt. Lucky for you, you can have the judgment removed from your credit report even before its expiry date. A civil judgment is the ruling that a court makes during a lawsuit. Judgments commonly occur due to unpaid collections. On your credit report, the judgments are there as public records. Anyone can see the public record and credit bureaus collect them to show your potential creditors your credit history. A judgment is among the worst things that can be on your credit report. It occurs when a court orders you to pay a debt. Situations that may lead to a judgment include failure to pay alimony, child support, and other small claim lawsuits. A judgment on your credit report lowers your credit score and potential lenders will not be quick to finance you because you are not likely to pay the debt, according to them. If you are lucky enough to get credit, you will pay high interest rates. A judgment will stay on your report for seven years. It will, therefore, have a negative impact on your score for seven years. However, its impact lessens with time. If you cannot imagine waiting that long, you can have it removed.

The Different Types of Judgment
Unsatisfied Judgment
This is the most damaging type of judgment. It occurs if you do not deal with the result of the lawsuit and you have not settled the debt.
Satisfied Judgment

This is a judgment that has been settled. It is wise to have your judgment satisfied by either paying it in full or negotiating a settlement.

Vacated Judgment

This is a judgment that has been dismissed through an appeal. This one should not be on your credit report.

Re-filed Judgment

This is a renewed judgment. This means it can keep showing up on your report even after the seven years.

Who Should You Pay to Satisfy Your Judgment?

Check your credit report to see who the current owner of the judgment is and how much you owe. Debts get sold and resold, so you must confirm. When an agency sues you, pay the debt quickly to avoid appearing before a judge. The worst mistake you can make is ignoring the lawsuit. If you do not show up for court, your lender wins by default. Also, make a point of talking to a legal professional so you know your options.

How to Delete A Judgment from Your Credit Report

Have the Court Validate the Judgment

Contact the court that issued the judgment through a validation letter, so they can verify the judgment. If the court does not bother or cannot verify, you can have the judgment removed. If the court sends a letter verifying the judgment, go through it with a fine-tooth comb, looking for inaccuracies. In case of any incorrect information, file a dispute with the bureaus. Or you contact a professional company to do all the work for you.

Chapter 19
How to Remove A Tax Lien from Your Credit Report

Tax liens are damaging, but not only to your credit. Tax liens result in tax levies; your property is seized by the government because of your tax debts. If this happens, you may end up losing your car, home, or bank accounts, depending on how big your debt is. Paid tax liens will stay on your report for seven years while unpaid tax liens can remain for an unspecified amount of time. Tax liens on your credit report are just like judgments. Both legally allow your lenders to collect their money from you. In the case of a tax lien, the IRS has legal rights to what you own. It could be real estate, personal property, business property, or financial assets. You cannot sell your home when you have a tax lien; neither can you qualify for new loans. The tax liens take priority in that if you sell your home, part of the money must be used to satisfy the tax lien. Creditors take tax liens very seriously and it makes them doubt your ability to repay debts. A tax lien can deduct 80-100 points from your credit score. If you have a higher score, the drop will be more severe. It is difficult to repair your credit after a tax lien because if it is unpaid, it will stay on your report, unlike other negative accounts that drop after seven years. The IRS is responsible for filing the tax liens but not directly reporting tax liens to the bureaus. The liens are public records just like judgments and bankruptcies. If you want to remove the tax lien from your report, you must deal with both the credit reporting agencies and the IRS. You are never notified that you have a tax lien until it has been put on your credit report. Bankruptcies do not discharge tax liens unless you file the bankruptcy before the tax lien is attached. Just like other debts, you have the legal right to dispute a tax lien. If the government is unable to prove the debt, you can have it removed from your report. The government is not quick to ignore disputes even when there are errors in the information. The IRS will either confirm or correct the information and the tax lien continues to stay on your report. If you satisfy the debt, the IRS will "release" it, but the paid tax lien will still be on your credit report for seven years. Fortunately, there is a way to dispute and have a tax lien removed from your report even when it is not fully satisfied. First, you need to request a "withdrawal". It is different from a "release" and you can request one while still paying the lien. You must continue with the payment plan and pay the full amount. This is a great option for someone trying to qualify for credit. To dispute and have the lien removed from your report, you must fill an IRS form 12277. You must work with the IRS and the three credit bureaus if you want the lien removed.

Chapter 20
How to Remove Credit Inquiries from Your Credit Report

Inquiries may remain on your report for two years. Whenever an inquiry is made, the three credit bureaus record it. Once the inquiry is logged, your credit score might be affected. At the bottom of your credit report is a "Credit Inquiries" section. When you apply for credit, your potential creditor checks your credit report to determine your creditworthiness—that is how an inquiry comes about. "New credit" makes up 10% of your credit score. How does it affect your score? New accounts: the number of new account types you have in various account categories affects your credit score. Student loans, mortgages and installment loans are more favorable than revolving credit. Number of recent inquiries: the amount of credit inquiries over the last two years is also considered. Time between inquiries: an inquiry negatively affects your score for 12 months after it was made and remains on the report for two years. Age of your account: an older credit account is better for your credit score than a new one. Inquiries are not as bad as delinquent debts or missed payments. Their effect on your score is low and lessens with time. If you have worse things on your credit report, focus on them first. Soft credit inquiries have no impact on your credit score while hard ones do. Applying for new credit such as a credit card, car loan, or mortgage results is a hard inquiry. A new cell phone, job application, and a new insurance policy can also result in a hard inquiry. Soft inquiries happen when a lender checks your report without your consent. Maybe you asked for a pre-approval rate but did not really apply for credit. A soft inquiry might also occur when an existing creditor checks your credit. Note: checking your own credit score or report is a soft inquiry. Sometimes inquiries will not have an impact on your credit score. In other circumstances, they will lead to a drop in your score with a maximum of 5 points. If you have many inquiries, the effect may be big. Too many inquiries at once also lead a potential lender to believe that you desperately need money and are in financial trouble. Avoid applying for numerous types of credit at the same time. However, while shopping around for a single type of loan, say an auto loan, and apply for a few of them to compare rates, they are counted as one when calculating your score. The same applies for a mortgage and credit cards. First, you need to get a copy of your report to see what is in your Credit Inquiries section. If you did not authorize an item and it is listed, you can dispute it by - Sending a letter to the creditor asking them to remove it because it was unauthorized. Hiring a professional to help repair your credit (especially if there are other negative accounts you need removed). To avoid unauthorized inquiries in future, place a freeze on your report.

Sample of A Credit Inquiry Removal Letter

Instead of standard mail delivery, send the letter via certified mail to increase the chances of a faster response. The letter should be personal and straight to the point. All the relevant information should be included.

Name
Address
Phone #
Credit bureau: Name
Credit bureau: Address
Date
Subject line

(Explain that you found an inquiry that you did not authorize. If you filed a dispute with the inquiry source, mention it. Request an investigation and an updated copy of your report reflecting the findings of the investigation).

Signature

Printed name

Include a copy of the report page that shows the inquiry. If possible, highlight the section with the error. If you want the bureau to hurry with the process, be as clear as you can. A less complicated dispute takes a shorter time to solve.

Chapter 21
Sample Credit Dispute Letter

If some of the information on your credit report is inaccurate, you can send a dispute letter to the three bureaus. You are also allowed to dispute "questionable" items. If you file a dispute, the bureaus are required by law to carry out an investigation and correct/verify the item failure to which they must delete it within 30 days. A dispute letter can also be sent to the creditor directly. Credit dispute letters are very effective—if you write them correctly. You can either do it yourself or involve a credit repair company. Can You Dispute Your Credit Report Online? Yes, you can. The three main credit bureaus have online forums on their sites. However, filing a dispute online is highly discouraged. You will have less control and limit your rights. Be sure to write the bureaus a hardcopy letter instead and retain copies for yourself as proof. The letter should be sent through certified mail and even go a step further and request a return receipt. Can You Dispute Your Report Over the Phone? Just like with online disputing, you can but it is better not to do it. What Items Can You Dispute? You can dispute anything on your report including, credit inquiries, bankruptcies, collections, personal information, repossessions, judgments, tax aliens, foreclosures, and charge offs. Be sure not to dispute positive accounts on your report. You will have a hard time getting them back once they are dropped. Who Should You Contact First, Your Creditor or The Bureaus? Experts recommend talking to your creditor first. After all, they sent the negative items. Contact them and try to settle the matter. Before calling them, have all the documents that support your claim, this includes evidence of the error (it could be a copy of your report or a letter from a collection agency). If you send copies of the paperwork, blackout your social security number and other sensitive information.

Writing A Credit Dispute Letter

Here are a few simple guidelines to remember when sending when drafting your dispute letter: The bureau knows the law. Avoid mentioning laws or threatening lawsuits. Be kind, aggressive language will only hurt you. Include copies of documents that support your claim (not original documents). The letter should be clear and concise.

Sample Credit Dispute Letter
Name
Address
City, St ZIP
Social security number: (your SS number)
Date of birth: (your D.O.B)
Experian
2220 Ritchey
Santa Ana, CA 92705
08/20/2018
Dear Credit Reporting Agency,

(Ask them to give proof that the item belongs on your report and that they have not violated your rights. If they cannot prove it, ask them to remove the item).

Account name
Account
Your confirmation Number
Name
TransUnion Dispute Address
TransUnion
P.O Box 1000
Chester, PA 19022
Experian Dispute Address

Experian
2220 Ritchey
Santa Ana, CA 92705
Equifax Dispute Address
Equifax
P.O Box 740241
Atlanta, GA 30374-0241

What If Your Creditor Does Not Follow Through? If your creditor does not respond, you will have to talk to the credit bureaus. Include a copy of the letter that you sent to your creditor in addition to the other documents. Include any phone conversations or mail response from the creditor as well. If the bureau does not respond, you might need legal help.

Chapter 22
Cease and Desist Letter for Debt Collectors

The unending phone calls from debt collectors can be annoying. They can even make you feel powerless. However, you can stop those letters and phone calls. You have a right, under the FDCPA, to ask a collection agency to stop contacting you and they must comply. This is a written form of communication that you send to a collection agency asking them to stop contacting you regarding a debt you owe. Your account number and personal contact information is included in the letter to clearly show the debt you are talking about. After receiving the letter, the agency can only contact you once concerning the debt. They can either write or call to inform you they will not try to collect the debt anymore and to respond to your request. This does not stop the debt collectors from using other methods to collect the debt. They can still sue you and place negative accounts on your credit report. Sending a cease and desist letter has two outcomes. The collector may stop trying to pursue the debt completely or they can file a lawsuit. The collection agency is likely to forego the debt if it is small and old (nearing the statute of limitations). On the other hand, the letter may provoke them to take a more drastic action, especially if the amount owed is significant. Let your language be firm, but professional. Avoid getting personal. Include your name, account, number, and address. Do not forget to reference the FDCPA. Be careful not to implicate yourself. Lastly, use certified mail to send the letter so you can be sure that they have received your letter. Retain a copy for yourself. If the calls do not stop after the agency has received your letter, talk to a credit repair company or an attorney.

A Cease and Desist Letter Sample
Your Name
Your Address
City, State, ZIP Code
Name of Collection Agency
Address of Collection Agency
City, State, ZIP Code of Collection Agency
Date
Re: Account Number
To (Collection Agency)
(Ask them to stop contacting you about any debt that you allegedly owe. Remember to reference the FDCPA here.

Tell them that if they continue with collection attempts, you will file a complaint with your state's attorney general's office and the Federal Trade Commission.

Let them know that if the communication continues you will pursue civil and criminal claims against the company. Make it clear that you have confirmed that they have received the letter).

Regards,
Your Name

If you do not want to send a cease and desist letter, you can ask the agency by phone to stop contacting you at your place of work. They must comply. Record this initial conversation in case they ignore the request. Avoid blocking the debt collector or disconnecting your phone because they may start contacting people close to you. Simply let the calls go to voicemail. Assign the number a silent ringtone.

Chapter 23
Sample Debt Validation Letter

The FDCPA (Fair Debt Collection Practices Act) offers you protection from debt collectors and offers you the right to ask for validation. A debt collection party consists of three primary parties: the original lender, the collection agency, and the consumer reporting agency or credit bureau. The collection agency and the creditor are both allowed to report a negative account to the credit bureau. The credit bureau files this information and sells it to your potential creditors so they can judge your financial responsibility. The FDCPA was passed by the federal government to offer protection to consumers against unfair practices and harassment by collection agencies. According to the act, a collection agency must stop contacting you if you tell them not to and they cannot call at odd hours. More importantly, the agencies must prove that they have a right to collect the debt and that the information is accurate. You can request for validation of the debt within 30 days after hearing from the collection agency. You are discouraged against contacting the agency directly because then, protection of your rights is not guaranteed. Sending a hard copy letter is the wise thing to do. Make the letter professional and concise. Avoid giving details about the debt (do not even admit to owning it or talk about your intentions not to pay). A mistake like this could reset the statute of limitations. In your letter, include the time the collection agency contacted you and the means of communication used. After that, make a request for the debt collector to validate the debt. Tell them of your intention to report to the relevant authorities should they fail to respond in time. Send the validation request via certified mail so that you can have proof that they received it. The collection agency is supposed to respond within 30 days; failure to which they cannot try to collect the debt anymore. If your debt is resold to another collection agency, you must send another validation letter the moment they contact you. Now, if the debt collector sends you validation, you can respond in several ways. One, you can choose to ignore the debt. The agency will continue with their collection attempts and your credit score will continue to suffer. The second option is to pay off the debt or come to an agreement with the agency. Before you rush to decide, confirm whether the debt is open or expired.

Sample of A Debt Validation Letter

To Whom It May Concern

(Say you are sending the letter to respond to the notice you received (give details) or a negative account on your credit report.

Make it clear that it is not a refusal to pay but you are acting on your rights. Also clarify that you are not asking for verification but validation. Ask for competent evidence that you are obligated by law to pay the debt to the agency. Let them know that they should respond within 30 days or have the negative accounts removed from your credit report. During the investigation period, you can ask them not to attempt to collect the debt).

Best Regards,

Your Name

Attach any documents that support your claims and all the necessary details.

Chapter 24
How to Deal with Debt Collection Agencies

Debt collection agencies can be annoying. Can you do anything about it? Read on to find out. A debt collection agency is a company that collects debts for creditors. They pressure you to pay the debt through letters, phone calls, and even lawsuits. The two major types of debt collectors include internal collection departments and third-party debt collectors. When your debt is 90 to 180 days due, you will most likely deal with internal collection departments—your original creditor. At this point, you can negotiate and come to an agreement. Once the 90 – 180 days are over, your creditor might sell your debt to a collection agency or contract them. The debt collectors can be ruthless and if you decide to negotiate with them, do it in writing. There are things that collection agencies are allowed or not allowed to do by the law. The FDCPA protects you from deceptive tactics and abuse from these agencies, even if you owe the debt. The collection agency can only talk to you, maybe your spouse, and your attorney about your debt. They can try to contact friends and family to get your contact information. They are not, however, allowed to harass them with phone calls. Can they withhold information regarding a debt? They cannot do that legally. They are supposed to write to you within 5 days since they first contacted you, notifying you of your right to file a dispute. It is your right to ask for the debt validation and information of the original creditor. Can they keep calling after you have asked them not to? A phone call telling them not to may not do it. Write to them instead. From there, they can only contact you once telling you of the action they will take. Can they keep harassing you for a debt you do not owe? No, they cannot. If the debt collector cannot verify the debt, they cannot make collection attempts. Can they garnish your wages? This depends on your state regulations. If your state does not allow it, the debt collector cannot threaten it—it is illegal. Can they ruin your credit? Collections agencies cannot damage your credit themselves but a collection account on your report can. If the debt is sold several times, you will end up with several collection accounts and this could be tragic to your score. Your Rights, As Far as Collection Agencies Are Concerned You have the following rights under the FDCPA. Debt validation, Coverage of all personal debts, Protection against harassment by debt collectors, Collection agencies are required to be totally honest, and Debt collectors cannot issue empty threats.

More Tips on How to Deal with Collection Agencies

Avoid talking to them via phone

If you must, record phone conversations with them

Do not believe them

Avoid negotiations or repayment during the validation process

Do not hide money

Avoid applying for new credit

Do not ignore the situation

Chapter 25
ChexSystems

ChexSystems are a lot like credit bureaus. They are used by banks to determine whether a new customer gets a checking account. However, they maintain and report information differently. It is not up to ChexSystems to decide to open an account for you; that is the bank's decision to make. Also, some banks do not use ChexSystems to make this decision. Being a consumer reporting agency, ChexSystems is governed by the FCRA (Federal Credit Reporting Act). The same way you have access to your credit report from the bureaus is the same way you can check your ChexSystems report. It will be difficult for you to open a checking account if, at some point, you had your account closed because of excessive overdrafts (OD), non-sufficient funds (NSF), suspected fraud, among other issues. To be clear, the problem will come about if you are still in debt to the bank. Banks get information about individuals with the above issues from ChexSystems. Your banking history may be the reason you are denied an account. ChexSystems stores information about bank accounts that were closed due to problems. Most of the banks in the U.S refer to ChexSystems during an account application process. If you are in their system, it means your account was closed "for cause". "For cause" here could mean: You provided false information on the account. Too many overdrafts over a short period of time. Not paying overdrafts or insufficient funds. Abuse of debit card, ATM transactions or savings account, Fraud, and Violation of rules and regulations. This list is not exhaustive; there are other reasons. When your account is closed for any of these reasons, you get into the ChexSystems' database. The information will be on record for five years. The scoring range for ChexSystems is 100 to 899. It is independent of the bureaus' scoring system. The fastest way is through the ChexSystems website. You can dispute inaccurate information just as with a credit report or place a system explaining a negative item. Whether you pay off the amount owed or not, the information remains on file. A paid overdraft will be updated but the information stays in the system for five years—unless you can prove that the account was improperly listed. If a bank denies you an account because of your ChexSystems report, you can freely access your report within 60 days. Not all banks use ChexSystems. You can look for one that does not and open an account there. Even then, they might want to see your credit report, Telecheck Data or Early Warning System (EWS). A bank that uses ChexSystems might also give you a "second chance", especially if you only have one or two incidents. You can also get an account, regardless of your ChexSystems record, if you agree to directly deposit your check (best for someone with a steady income). Make sure you check the bank's policies before you try to open an account with them. Alternatively, get a prepaid debit card. You can load funds on to it and use it for payments, just like a checking account.

Chapter 26
How to Request Debt Validation from Debt Collectors

You have the right to request for "debt validation" under the FDCPA. You can demand that the creditor prove that the debt is your responsibility. A collection agency must provide proof that they are legally allowed to collect the debt. After receiving your letter, a collection agency must stop trying to collect the debt until they properly validate the debt. There is no specified time limit for validating a debt; but if they have not provided the necessary information, they cannot make collection attempts. Instead of validating the debt, a debt collector can resell the debt to your original creditor. Sometimes, a debt collector may not have all the required information to collect the debt. Other times, they may continue harassing you even after you have settled the account with your original creditor. In other cases, you may not owe the debt they are trying to collect. A debt validation helps with all these. Here is a real-life example to help you understand debt collection. Mary borrowed money from Tom. After some time, she receives a call from Lisa asking for $1000 in payment of Tom's debt. How will Mary know for sure that she owes Lisa $1000 instead of Tom? When she pays Lisa the money, will her debt to Tom be satisfied? This is the kind of information that a debt validation seeks to confirm. You will know the legal owner of the debt and the accuracy of the information. Failure to seek validation may see you pay a higher amount, the wrong person, or a debt you do not owe. The FDCPA gives you the right to validate a debt due to the reasons above. If a debt collector fails to validate a debt, it cannot continue to be on your credit report. A debt validation letter asks the collection agency to prove its legal ownership to the debt, that you agreed to the owed amount, and that all the other information is correct.

5 Steps to Validating Your Debt

Step 1

When a collection agency first contacts you about a debt, send them a written validation request via certified mail within 30 days. Certified mail gives you proof that your letter has been received. Make sure you keep a personal copy of the letter. After receiving this letter, a collection agency can only continue to try and collect the debt if they supply validation.

Step 2

If the collection agency does not respond, send them the validation request letter, a copy of the receipt and another letter saying that you will not repay the amount in accordance to the FDCPA.

Step 3

If the debt collector still sends a notice of the debt to a credit bureau without validating it, the notice must be removed. Notify the credit reporting agencies of the validation failure.

Step 4

If the debt collector validates the debt, then the debt is yours and they can go on with the collection attempts. Also, make sure the debt has not reached the statute of limitations. When a debt has been verified, you can either satisfy it or negotiate a settlement. You can also ask for a pay for delete. Note: do not try to ignore the debt.

Chapter 27
Disputing Credit Card Charges

Is there a time you were charged for something you never received or a product you returned? Have you been charged twice for one item? All these errors are frustrating, but you can correct them. You only need to be a little patient and understand the dispute settlement procedures put in place by the FCBA (Fair Credit Billing Act). The regulation covers revolving charge accounts such as department store accounts and "open end" credit accounts such as credit cards. Installment contracts are not covered. The settlement procedures by the FCBA are for billing errors only. These include but are not limited to: Bills not being sent to your correct address—the creditors should have your address change in writing, 20 days before the end of the billing period. Math errors. When credits and payments are not posted. Charges for merchandise you rejected. Wrong amount or date on charges. Unauthorized charges. Exercise Your Rights - The law offers consumer protection and to take advantage of it you must: Send a letter to the creditor's billing enquiries address. Do not use the address that you use to send your payments. In the letter include your account number, address, name, and a clear description of the error. Your letter should get to the creditor no later than 60 days after they mailed the first wrong bill. Make sure you send it by certified mail and request a return receipt. This way, you will have proof. Support your stand with copies of relevant documents (do not send originals). Have a copy of the dispute letter with you. The creditor is required to acknowledge the complaint within 30 days in writing—unless the issue has been taken care of. The dispute must be solved within two billing cycles from the time they get your letter. When the investigation is ongoing, you can withhold payments on the amount with issues. Other parts of the bill should be paid, though, and that includes financial charges on the amount in question. It is against the law for the creditor to try and collect the amount in question and any related charges if the investigation is still in progress. They can, however, apply the disputed amount against your limit. The creditor can report that you raised the challenge, but they cannot discriminate against you or threaten to take any action. If your issue is found to be valid, the creditor has to offer you an explanation in writing. Any late fees, and finance charges concerning the error must be removed. If they find the bill to be correct, they must write to you explaining what you owe and the reasons. Complaints Concerning the Quality of Products - These are not considered billing errors. But you can go about the issue the same way you would against any seller, according to state laws.

Additional Billing Rights

Issuers of "open end" credit must:

Offer you a notice in writing whenever you open an account.

Send you a statement for every billing period.

Send bills 21 days before they are due.

Refund or credit overpayments promptly.

Chapter 28
Statute of Limitations on Debt Collection

Collection agencies usually care more about getting paid than they do about their collection methods. It is your responsibility to know your rights and understand how you can deal with them. The statute of limitations protects you from very old debt. In most cases, the statute of limitations is seven years, or less. Even if you owe the debt, be on your toes because collection agencies do not have your best interest at heart. You should know about the laws and rules that regulate debt collection. Collection agencies can try anything to make you pay up what you owe them. A consumer may be pushed to pay off a debt because it is on their credit report. However, you do not really have to pay a debt just because it is on your report. There are four common types of debt and each one is treated differently.

Oral Contracts

You are obliged by an oral agreement to pay off this kind of debt, even though there is no written agreement.

Written Contracts

A written contract is simply that; a contract in writing, showing the amount owed. Both the creditor and the debtor have a written agreement, signed by the two parties.

Promissory Notes

It is a brief statement of the terms and agreements and is considered a negotiable instrument. They usually contain a "promise to pay" and how the payment will be done. A mortgage is an example of a promissory note.

Revolving Line of Credit

This is a credit line for a debtor to use at their discretion. The terms of repayment and the amount vary depending on market conditions, a person's history, and creditworthiness. A HELOC (home equity line of credit) and a credit card are good examples of a revolving line of credit.

Note: the statute of limitations varies from one state to another.

Knowing the Jurisdiction of Your Credit Card Debt

Where you applied for the credit card determines the jurisdiction under which your credit card falls—in most cases. In other cases, the state in which you live is the determinant. You can argue the state's statute that should be used and why.

Is Your Debt Past the Statute of Limitations?

Step 1

Determine the date of last activity, that is, when you last paid or the first time you received a letter demanding payment for an overdue debt.

Step 2

Find out your state's statute of limitations. From the current year, subtract the year of the last activity and see if the creditor can collect the debt. Should You Make A Partial Payment? Even with an expired statute of limitations, you may think it is noble to pay off the debt since you borrowed it. But before you do, know the implications. Making a payment restarts the clock on your debt. You admit to owning the debt. Collection attempts may resume, and you can even get sued. Note: whether a debt collector can continue with collection attempts after the statute of limitations has expired depends on the laws of your state. They can also sue you, but the expired statute of limitations may help your defense. Delinquent debts stay on your report for seven years. Even if the statute of limitations in your state is less than seven years, the debt will remain on your report even after it has expired.

Chapter 29
The Fair Debt Collection Practices Act

The FDCPA (Fair Debt Collection Practices Act) was first passed in 1978 to offer protection to consumers and place regulations on debt collectors' tactics. The FDCPA protects you from collection agencies' shady debt collection practices and gives you the right to fight back. You can use it to get debt collectors out of your life and have collection accounts dropped from your credit report. You can even sue them. The right to ask for debt validation is one of the most important tools that the FDCPA gives consumers. If a debt collector contacts you about a debt and you are not sure whether you owe it or not, you can send them a debt validation letter. According to the FDCPA, you also have the right to determine how frequently and even when a debt collector may contact you. The FDCPA is very clear on what debt collectors can and cannot do. They cannot: Try to collect more than you owe. Debt collectors are notorious for squeezing in additional fees contrary to the original agreement. Keep calling you repeatedly throughout the day. The law prohibits creditors from calling you anytime between 8:00 a.m. and 9:00 p.m. or any other inconvenient time. Use intimidating or abusive language. Collection agencies cannot threaten you with physical violence or insult you over the phone. Talk to other people regarding your debt. The only people that a debt collector can discuss your debt with include close family members (parent or spouse) and legal advisors. Ignore a debt validation letter. When a creditor receives a debt validation letter, they cannot attempt to collect a debt; not before they respond to your letter. What Are the Main Complaints Against Debt Collectors? Collection agencies still violate the law. These are the primary complaints against them: Harassing an alleged debtor or other people. Demanding more than the law permits. Threatening consumers with dire consequences. Calling a consumer's place of work without permission. Revealing debt details to other people. Not sending required consumer notice. Not verifying disputed debts. Contacting an alleged debtor after getting a "cease communication" notice. Suing A Creditor, Credit Bureau or Collection Agency in Small Claims Court. The fine for each violation is $1,000 and the money is rewarded to you. Suing them might also serve as a lesson and prevent them from harassing others.

Reasons for suing a creditor:
Failure to report a disputed debt
Pulling your report without permission
Reporting wrong information
Reasons for suing a credit bureau:
Not correcting information after receiving proof
Re-reporting an item that was dropped from your report without sending you a written notification within five days
Not responding to a written dispute (they should respond within 30 days)
Reasons for suing a debt collector:
Trying to be both an assignee and purchaser of an account
Misrepresenting themselves
Trying to re-age an account
Not reporting a disputed debt
Not validating a debt then continuing with collection attempts
Calling after receiving a cease and desist letter
Reporting n debt that is not validated
Calling at inconvenient hours
Calling third parties regarding your debt
Threats to garnish your wages
Harassing you

Chapter 30
Authorized User

If you are in the process of building your credit score, being authorized to use another person's card can be effective. It may not be the same as establishing a credit history of your own, but it will help improve your score. However, there is a flip side. If the original credit card holder is not responsible with their payments, your credit could be hurt. Before making such an important decision, here are few things you need to know. When you are an authorized user on someone else's card, you can use the card in your name. You will make purchases and other payments using the credit card, just as you would with your own card. To become an authorized user, the credit card holder will have to add your name to their account to give you permission to use it. You will be given a credit card associated with the account, but your privileges will be limited. For instance, in most cases, you cannot make any adjustments to the account, such as adding more users or asking for a credit increase. Being an authorized user, you have no legal obligation to make any credit card bill payments or satisfy any debts associated with it. When you are an authorized user, your credit will be affected in a few ways. The account will most likely be on your credit reports—not all credit card companies report authorized users' activities. Make sure you know whether they do in advance. If the account will be on your report, the actions of the primary account holder will affect your credit, either positively or negatively. If he/she has a long, positive payment history, your score will improve. A low utilization rate is also good. The opposite happens if the account holder makes a late payment or misses it altogether. A high rate of credit utilization will hurt your credit score too. The person you choose must be trustworthy and financially responsible. This is a decision that you must be very strategic while making. Being an authorized user can really help your score but if the primary account holder is irresponsible, your score will suffer terribly. Note: having an authorized user does not affect the primary account holder's score, even if you have a poor credit history. Some credit card companies allow for the opening of a joint credit card account. The main difference between being a joint account holder and an authorized user is that a joint account holder has more responsibilities. You will be legally obligated to make payments and pay off debts. The process of being added is also more complicated. It is almost the same as applying for your own credit card. Joint accounts are commonly used by spouses while the authorized user tactic is mostly for parents who are helping their kids establish credit.

Chapter 31
Credit Card Piggybacking

Building credit can be difficult. If you have no payment history, creditors will not be quick to lend you money. A credit card builder loan or a secured credit card can help you establish credit. However, you might also want to know about "piggybacking" credit. This is when you become an authorized user on another person's credit card for the purpose of building your credit. This strategy might not work because some credit card issuers do not report the activities of an authorized user to credit bureaus. If you are completely new to credit, your first piggybacking option is a significant other, close friend or a parent who is financially responsible. Sometimes, however, you do not have these options; then what? Over the past few years, credit piggybacking services have come up. When you apply for these services, you will be made an authorized user on a stranger's credit card for a fee. So, what should you opt for? In most cases, piggybacking will not go according to plan, but it can boost your credit a little. You may be disappointed to learn that some credit card companies will not report your activities and if they do, it will be in an unpredictable way. Sometimes, your positive history will go to the original cardholder's report and not your own. If you do not want to face any of these difficulties, consult the credit card company and see if and how they report your activity. Many people will not easily make you an authorized user on their card. What if your irresponsible financial habits damage their score? However, you also need to be choosy. If the cardholder pays their bills on time and has low credit card utilization, your credit will be positively affected. If their irresponsible spending negatively impacts your score, you can ask the credit card issuer to take your name off the account and request the bureaus to remove the account from your report.

Types of Credit Piggybacking

Traditional Piggybacking

With this type of piggybacking, you talk to a trusted relative or friend and ask them to make you an authorized user on their credit card. Their credit card payment history will start to appear on your reports. You might not even have to use the card yourself for this to work.

For-profit Piggybacking

There are companies that can help you piggyback on another person's card. The two people being paired up are usually strangers and you must pay a fee. This type of piggybacking can be risky. It is wise to be added only if you trust the account holder; except it is not easy to trust a stranger. Is it worth it? FICO discourages this type of piggybacking. The FICO Score 8 model reduces the benefits of tradeline renting. For-profit piggybacking could also make you an easy target for ID theft because when applying, you must disclose much of your personal information.

Chapter 32
How to Use Goodwill Letters in Credit Repair

Having accounts eliminated from your report plays an important role in credit repair. You can use the dispute process for accounts that are past the credit reporting time limit or those that do not belong to you. For the most part, however, this process is challenging and does not result in success. You can have a negative account removed by offering "pay for delete" or paying off the balance. If you have cleared the debt already, this will not work as leverage. Your other option is a goodwill letter. A goodwill letter, just as the name suggests, is one that you address to your creditors and ask them to remove negative accounts from your report. They are not under any obligation to remove correct information, but some will not mind doing it, especially if your credit history is good and you only have several late payments. Keep your goodwill letter simple and short. Tell them the account you want removed, talk of the payments you have made on time and explain briefly why you missed payments. Ask them to update your report as a courtesy. Do not blame or accuse the creditor and use a polite, pleasant tone.

Send the letter as an email or to the address of the creditor—usually indicated on the credit report or recent billing statements. If you cannot find an address on your credit report or they do not reply in 7-10 business days, find another address on their website. A creditor may remove the account and update your report when they receive your goodwill letter. On the other hand, they may tell you that they are not legally allowed to remove the information. Look at myFICO forums for successful goodwill letters. Instead of explicitly asking the creditor to delete negative information, they ask for a "goodwill adjustment". Asking a creditor to remove information may violate their agreement with credit bureaus. Some people prefer to make a call instead of writing a letter. However, the calls are answered by customer service representatives. They do not have any authority to update your credit report. Try to reach someone at a higher position.

Chapter 33
Sample Pay for Delete Letter for Credit Report Cleanup

When you want a creditor to remove negative information from your report, you can use the pay for delete negotiation strategy. This strategy works if you owe the debt and cannot dispute it. Learn how to send a successful pay for delete letter below. Tips for Sending a Pay for Delete Letter - First, you may want to send out a debt validation letter before your pay for delete offer on debt collection. That is, if 30 days have not passed since the collector first contacted you. Debt collectors are obligated to send you proof of the debt. If they do not have enough proof of the debt, they are not allowed to report the debt to a credit reporting company or collect the debt from you. But as soon as they verify the debt, they can continue with the collection activity. Sometimes, sending a pay for delete is not necessary—especially if it no longer appears on your report or it will be deleted from the report in a few years. In a case like this, you are better off waiting for it to fall off the report after expiration of the credit reporting time limit. When that happens, it will no longer influence your credit score.

Only send a pay for delete letter if you know you will pay the full listed amount immediately the collector or creditor accepts your offer. In many instances, the collector or creditor will request that you pay the full amount within a specified timeframe—typically several business days. They can also annul the acceptance of the offer and resume collection actions if you do not pay in time. When sending the letter and follow-up payment, use certified mail and ask for a return receipt. This will give you proof that you mailed the letter and payment and that they were received. Have a copy of the pay for delete letter for record purposes. It may also help if you decide to use the strategy in future with another collector. What If They Reject Your Pay for Delete Offer? The creditor is under no obligation to accept your offer. It is nothing more than a request that can be rejected. If they reject your offer, you have the following options: Pay off the debt anyway. It is better to have a zero balance than any other amount. Pay an amount that is less than the due balance. Give a settlement offer and see whether the collector or creditor will accept it. Wait for another collector to take over the account and then make them a settlement or pay for a delete offer. Do not pay the debt. Wait for the reporting limit to expire and for the item to fall off the report. Collection efforts will not stop. You can prevent third-party collectors from calling you with a cease and desist letter. Also, you may get sued for your debt.

Conclusion

Society relies heavily on credit for most financial decisions. Today, good credit is not just important for getting a loan or a credit card. Many businesses must check your credit before deciding whether they will extend their products and services to you. Mortgage lenders need to be sure that you will pay your mortgage responsibly before they can finance you. Without good credit, the mortgage lender concludes that giving you a loan is risky for them. If they still approve, regardless of your poor credit, they will charge you a very high interest rate. Bad credit will see you pay a higher mortgage amount or worse, your mortgage application will be declined. Just because you are not currently interested in buying a house does not mean that your credit does not matter. Landlords will, in most cases, consult your credit before renting you a house or apartment. Your lease is considered a loan. You require a loan to purchase a car unless you have the full amount at hand. Your credit score affects the loan amount and interest rate and whether you will be given the loan in the first place. With excellent credit, you will qualify for a higher loan amount and the interest rate will be lower. A poor credit score translates to limited options. Not many lenders will be ready to finance you and the few that will be willing might charge a very high interest rate. You will, therefore, must pay more money for the car. During the hiring process, many employers also run credit checks. They check the credit reports, not the scores. A potential employer might not consider you if your report shows financial irresponsibility. Your debt level might even be considered too high for the offered salary. There are employers that also check your scores before they give a raise or promotion, especially if the position is finance related. A good number of people dream of starting a business of their own. But to start a business you may need a lot of cash that you do not even have. If that is the case, you will have no option but to get a small business loan; and as you already know, you need to have good credit for that. Many people have no idea, but your credit is required to establish utility services. For instance, according to the electricity company, you are borrowing a month of service. Before they can turn on the electricity for you, they need to know that your credit is good. The same goes for other utility companies. Your payment history defines your credit. Therefore, many businesses determine future financial responsibility by checking your credit. Because of these and many other reasons, having good credit is important and should be a priority to you.

Be sure you are sending your dispute to the right credit bureau (whichever one issued the report you are trying to correct). The addresses of each of the three major bureaus are:

Equifax Information Services LLC
P.O. Box 740256
Atlanta, GA 30374-0256
Experian
P.O. Box 4500
Allen, TX 75013
TransUnion Consumer Solutions
P.O. Box 2000
Chester, PA 19016-2000

Sample Letter for Disputing Errors on Your Credit Report

You may want to enclose a copy of your report with the items in question circled.

Send your letter by certified mail, "return receipt requested," so you can document what the credit reporting company received. Remember to include copies of the applicable enclosures and save copies for your files.

[Your Name]
[Your Address]
[Your City, State, Zip Code]
[Date]
Complaint Department
[Company Name]
[Street Address]
[City, State, Zip Code]
Dear Sir or Madam:

I am writing to dispute the following information in my file. I have circled the items I dispute on the attached copy of the report I received.

This item [identify item(s) disputed by name of source, such as creditors or tax court, and identify type of item, such as credit account, judgment, etc.] is [inaccurate or incomplete] because [describe what is inaccurate or incomplete and why]. I am requesting that the item be removed [or request another specific change] to correct the information.

Enclosed are copies of [use this sentence if applicable and describe any enclosed documentation, such as payment records and court documents] supporting my position. Please reinvestigate this [these] matter[s] and [delete or correct] the disputed item[s] as soon as possible.

Sincerely,

Your name

Sample Letter for Disputing a Debit Card Charge

Use this sample to draft a letter disputing a debit card charge.

[Date]
[Your Name]
[Your Address, City, State, Zip Code]
[Your Account Number]

[NAME OF DEBIT CARD Issuer]
[Billing Inquiries]
[Address, City, State, Zip Code]

DEAR SIR OR MADAM:

I am writing to dispute a debit in the amount of [$_____] on my account. The amount is inaccurate because the merchandise I ordered was not delivered. I ordered the merchandise on [date]. The seller promised to deliver the merchandise to me on [date], but I never got it. [If appropriate, include: When I placed my order, the seller did not tell me my account would be debited before shipping.]

I am requesting that the error be corrected, that any finance charges related to the disputed amount be credited to my account, and that I get an accurate statement.

Enclosed are copies of [use this sentence to describe any enclosed information, like sales slips, payment records, documentation of shipment or delivery dates] supporting my position and experience. Please correct the debiting error promptly.

SINCERELY,
    [Your name]

Sample Letter for Disputing Billing Errors

Use this sample to draft a letter disputing billing errors.
[Date]
[Your Name]
[Your Address]
[Your City, State, Zip Code]
[Your Account Number]
[Name of Creditor]
[Billing Inquiries]
[Address]
[City, State, Zip Code]
Dear Sir or Madam:

I am writing to dispute a billing error in the amount of [$_____] on my account. The amount is inaccurate because [describe the problem]. I am requesting that the error be corrected, that any finance and other charges related to the disputed amount be credited as well, and that I receive an accurate statement.

Enclosed are copies of [use this sentence to describe any information you are enclosing, like sales slips or payment records] supporting my position. Please investigate this matter and correct the billing error as soon as possible.

Sincerely,
[Your name]

Sample Consumer Complaint Letter

Use this sample to draft a complaint about a product or service. Want help resolving a consumer problem? Check out these tips and strategies.

[Your Address]
[Your City, State, Zip Code]
[Date]
[Name of Contact Person]
[Title]
[Company Name]
[Street Address]
[City, State, Zip Code]
Dear [Contact Person]:

On [date], I bought [or had repaired] a [name of the product with the serial or model number or service performed]. I made this purchase at [location, date, and other important details of the transaction].

Unfortunately, your product has not performed well [or the service was inadequate] because [state the problem].

To resolve the problem, I would appreciate your [state the specific action you want]. Enclosed are copies [copies, not originals] of my records [receipts, guarantees, warranties, cancelled checks, contracts, model and serial numbers, and any other documents] concerning this purchase/repair.

I look forward to your reply and a resolution to my problem. I will wait [set a time limit] before seeking third-party assistance. Please contact me at the above address or by phone [home or office numbers with area codes].

Sincerely,

[Your Name]
[Account Number]

Sample Letter for Disputing Errors on Your Credit Report with Information Providers

Your letter should identify each item you dispute, state the facts, and explain why you dispute the information, and ask that the information provider take action to have it removed or corrected. You may want to enclose a copy of your report with the item(s) in question circled.

Send your letter by certified mail, "return receipt requested," so you can document what the information provider received. Remember to include copies of the applicable enclosures and save copies for your files.

[Your Name]
[Your Address]
[Your City, State, Zip Code]
[Date]

COMPLAINT DEPARTMENT
[Company Name]
[Street Address]
[City, State, Zip Code]

I am writing to dispute the following information that your company provided to [give the name of the credit reporting company whose report has incorrect information]. I have circled the items I dispute on the attached copy of the credit report I received.

This item [identify item(s) disputed by type of item, such as credit account, judgment, etc., and your account number or another method for the information provider to locate your account] is [inaccurate or incomplete] because [describe what is inaccurate or incomplete and why]. I am requesting that [name of company] have the item(s) removed [or request another specific change] to correct the information.

Enclosed are copies of [use this sentence if applicable and describe any enclosed documents, such as payment records and court documents] supporting my position. Please reinvestigate this [these] matter[s] and contact the national credit reporting companies to which you provided this information to have them [delete or correct] the disputed item[s] as soon as possible.

Sincerely,

Your name

Sample Pay for Delete Letter

Your Name
Your Address Your City, State Zip
Collector's Name
Collector's Address
Collector's City, State Zip
Date
Re: Account Number XXXX-XXXX-XXXX-XXXX
Dear Collection Manager:

This letter is in response to your [letter / call / credit report entry] on [date] related to the debt referenced above. I wish to save us both some time and effort by settling this debt.

Please be aware that this is not an acknowledgment or acceptance of the debt, as I have not received any verification of the debt. Nor is this a promise to pay and is not a payment agreement unless you provide a response as detailed below.

I am aware that your company can report this debt to the credit bureaus as you deem necessary. Furthermore, you can change the listing since you are the information furnisher.

I am willing to pay [this debt in full / $XXX as settlement for this debt] in return for your agreement to remove all information regarding this debt from the credit reporting agencies within ten calendar days of payment. If you agree to the terms, I will send certified payment in the amount of $XXX payable to [Collection Agency] in exchange to have all information related to this debt removed from all my credit files.

If you accept this offer, you also agree not to discuss the offer with any third-party, excluding the original creditor. If you accept the offer, please prepare a letter on your company letterhead agreeing to the terms. This letter should be signed by an authorized agent of [Collection Agency]. The letter will be treated as a contract and subject to the laws of my state.

As granted by the Fair Debt Collection Practices Act, I have the right to dispute this alleged debt. If I do not receive your postmarked response within 15 days, I will withdraw the offer and request full verification of this debt.

Please forward your agreement to the address listed above.

Sincerely,

Your Name

Sample Goodwill Letter

Here is a template goodwill letter for missed payments on a credit card:
[your name]
[your address]
Account Number: [your account number]
[date]
To Whom It May Concern:
Thank you for taking the time to read this letter. I am writing because I noticed that my most recent credit report contains [a late payment/payments] reported on [date/dates] for my [name of account] account.

I want you to know that I understand my financial obligations, and if it were not for [circumstance that caused you to miss a payment], I'd have an excellent repayment record. I made a mistake in falling behind, but since then, [description of how your circumstances have changed or how you have improved your money management]. Since then, I have had a spotless record of on-time payments.

I'm planning to apply for [a mortgage/auto loan/etc.], and it's come to my attention that the missed payment on my record could hurt my ability to qualify. I truly believe that it does not reflect my creditworthiness and commitment to repaying my debts. It would help me immensely if you could give me a second chance and make a goodwill adjustment to remove the late [payment/payments] on [date/dates].

Thank you for your consideration, and I hope you will approve my request.

Best,

[your name]

Late Payment Goodwill Adjustment Sample Letter to Creditor

[Date]
[Your Name]
[Your Address]
[Your Phone Number]
[Your Email Address]
[Your Account Number]
Complaint Department
[Name of Creditor]
[Creditor Address]

Dear Sir or Madam:

I hope you are doing well today. My name is [your name], and I have been a satisfied customer of [creditor] for [number] of years. I have always made my payments on time, but unfortunately, I recently made a mistake on [date].

I understand how important it is to make timely payments. However, I missed my payment because [brief explanation of why you missed your payment]. But I am confident this will not happen again. As you can see from my account history, I have a long record of on-time payments before and since the late payment.

As a courtesy, I respectfully request that you make a goodwill adjustment to remove the late payment on [date]. Please consider my track record as proof that I take my financial obligations seriously.

If you have any questions, or if you would like to speak with me in more detail, please call me at [your phone number] or send me an email at [your email address here].

Thank you for your consideration,

[Your name]

Sample Credit Report Dispute Letter

Date
Your Name
Your Address, City, State, Zip Code
Your Phone Number and Email
Complaint Department
Name of Company
Credit Bureau Address
City, State, Zip Code
Dear Sir or Madam:

I recently obtained a copy of my credit report from your agency and found the following item to be in error:

Item 1: I dispute the unpaid balance on [ABC credit card] account number [555111]. This account has been paid in full as of [date].

I am requesting that the item be [removed, updated, or other suggested change] to correct the information.

Enclosed are copies of [use this statement if you have bank statements, canceled checks, or other documentation] supporting my position. Please investigate this matter and (delete or correct) the disputed item(s) as soon as possible.

Sincerely,

YOUR NAME
Enclosures: [List the documents you are enclosing. If none, do not include this section].

Failure to Respond to Deletion/Correction Letter

[Your name]
  [Your return address]
[Date]
[Debt collector name]
[Debt collector Address]
Re: [Account number for the debt if you have it]
Dear debt collector,

I am responding to your contact about collecting a debt. You contacted me by [phone/mail], on [date]

and identified the debt as [any information they gave you about the debt].

I do not have any responsibility for the debt you are trying to collect.

If you have good reason to believe that I am responsible for this debt, mail me the documents that make

you believe that. Stop all other communication with me and with this address, and record that I dispute

having any obligation for this debt. If you stop your collection of this debt, and forward or return it to

another company, please indicate to them that it is disputed. If you report it to a credit bureau (or have

already done so), also report that the debt is disputed.

Thank you for your cooperation.

Sincerely,

[Your name] – sign

Sample Letter for Removing Credit Inquiries

Name
Address
Phone #
Credit Bureau: Name
Credit Bureau: Address
Date
RE: Request Investigation of Credit Inquiry on My Behalf
Dear Sir or Ma'am,

I recently conducted a review of my credit report, and I noticed that your agency showed two (2) credit inquiries that I find to be problematic.

The first inquiry in question was apparently made by Company X on May 2nd, 2016 and I have no recollection of doing any business with Company X.

I contacted Company X and asked them to take action to get this inquiry removed from their records and to erase any record of the inquiry with all credit reporting agencies. They assured me they would comply with my request and take whatever steps necessary to resolve the issue, but I wanted to contact you as well, just to make sure this gets done.

The second inquiry was made by Company Y. I do remember working with Company Y, as they are the company, I used for my recent auto loan. However, I applied for that loan just a few weeks after applying for similar loans from Company W and Company Z. Based on my research, I believe only Company Y, W, or Z should be showing on my report.

Please investigate these inquiries at your earliest possible convenience, as I am going to be applying for a home mortgage soon. I would very much like to ensure my credit score is showing an accurate depiction of my creditworthiness.

Please update me with a full report on your findings within the next two weeks. I look forward to having this situation rectified as soon as possible.

Thanks for your prompt attention to this matter,

Signature

Printed Name

Pay for Delete Sample Letter

Creditor

Your Name
　　Your Address
Your City, State Zip
Collection Agency's Name
Collection Agency's Address
Collection Agency's City, State Zip
Date
Re: Account Number XXXX-XXXX-XXXX-XXXX
Dear Collection Specialist:

　　I am writing this letter in response to your recent correspondence related to the account number I referenced in the subject line above. I am considering the possibility of settling this debt.

　　I accept no responsibility for ownership of this debt. However, I am willing to compromise. I can offer a significant settlement amount in exchange for the following:

　　You agree, in writing, to designate the account as "payment in full" once you are in receipt of the agreed upon payment amount. The account will not be designated as a "paid collection" or "settled account."

　　You agree, in writing, to completely remove all references to this account from all credit bureaus to which you report.

　　I am willing to pay the <full balance owed / $XXX as settlement for this debt> in exchange for your agreement to remove all information regarding this debt from all credit reporting agencies to which you report within fifteen calendar days of receipt of payment.

When I am in receipt of a signed agreement with the terms from an authorized representative on your company letterhead, I will pay $XXX via cashier's check/wire transfer/money order.

If I do not receive your response to this offer within fifteen calendar days, I will rescind this offer and follow up with a method of verification letter.

Please forward your agreement to the address listed above at your earliest convenience, as I look forward to resolving this matter quickly.

Sincerely,

Your Name

Frivolous-Letter Rejection

This is written after 30 days of no response from the credit bureaus.

Date
Name
Address
Credit Bureau
Bureau Address
RE: Dispute Letter of date you sent in first or subsequent requests
To Whom it May Concern,

This letter is formal notice that you have failed to respond to my dispute letter of (date). I sent this letter registered mail and have enclosed a copy of the return receipt which you signed on (date).

As you are aware, federal law requires you to respond within 30 days. It has now been over that period since the receipt of my letter. As you are no doubt aware, failure to comply with federal regulations by credit reporting agencies are in serious violation of the Fair Credit Reporting Act and may be investigated by the FTC. Obviously, I am maintaining detailed records of all my correspondence with you.

I am aware that you may have misplaced my letters or have failed to respond to my letter because of an oversight due to the high volume of the requests you receive daily. If this is the case, I am sure you'll want to handle this matter as soon as possible. For this purpose, I have included a copy of my original request, the dated receipt of your reception of the original letter and a copy of the proof verifying the incorrectness of the credit item you have mistakenly placed on my records.

The following information therefore needs to be verified and deleted from the report as soon as possible:

CREDITOR AGENCY - Account #123-34567-ABC

Please delete this erroneous item from my credit report as soon as possible.

Sincerely,

Your Signature

Bankruptcy/Charge Offs Accounts Not Identified

Today's Date]
[Original creditor name (or name of collection agency if account was sold)
Creditor address
Creditor City, State, ZIP]
To Whom It May Concern:
In a recent review of my credit report, I have noticed some errors. Please make the following changes:
[Account name], account # [account number]
Example 1: The Date of First Delinquency with original creditor is not provided. Please provide this.
Example 2: The end of the seven-year reporting is not listed. Please provide this.
Example 3: Credit Limit is not listed. Please provide this.
Example 4: Date of Major Delinquency is not listed. Please provide this.
Example 5: Actual Payment Amount is incorrect. Please correct or remove this.
[Account name], account # [account number]
Example 6: The Date of Major Delinquency is not listed. Please provide this.
Example 7: Charge Off Amount is not provided. Please provide this.
Example 8: Incorrect Account Status. Please correct or remove this.
If you cannot verify the details and/or provide the requested information, kindly remove these damaging accounts from my credit

report. If you can verify the information you have listed as accurate, please provide the name of the person supplying this data as well as the manner in which it was provided in order that I may pursue additional remedies.

Sincerely,
[Your Name
Your Address
Your City, STATE ZIP]

Credit Bureau Late Payment Dispute Sample Letter

[Date]
[Your Name]
[Your Address]
SSN: [Your Social Security number]
Complaint Department
[Name of Credit Bureau]
[Credit Bureau Address]
Dear Sir or Madam:

I am writing to dispute the following information in my credit file. The item I am disputing is [insert account name and number], as reported by [insert lender]. (Optional) This account is also circled on the attached credit report.

This delinquent account record is inaccurate because [describe why the late payment was reported]. I am requesting that the account be corrected to show that it has always been current, with no record of being delinquent.

(Optional) I have included copies of my credit report, [list any other documents included]. The file number of this credit report is [insert credit report file number or ID number].

Please investigate this matter and correct the disputed item as soon as possible.

Sincerely,
[Your name]
Enclosures: [List what you are enclosing]

Credit Freeze Letter

Your name
   Mailing address
Date
To [send one letter to each of the bureaus]:
Equifax Security Freeze, P.O. Box 740241, Atlanta, GA 30374-0241
Experian: P.O. Box 9532, Allen, TX 75013
TransUnion: P.O. Box 6790, Fullerton, CA 92834-6790
Dear Sir or Madam:
My name is _____ and I would like to place a security freeze on my file.
My current address is: _____
My prior address was (if within last two years): _____
My Social Security number is: _____
My birthday is: _____MM/DD/YYYY
I have included proof of my current address and proof of my identity [copy of state-issued ID card or
driver's license].
I am a victim of identity theft and have enclosed a copy of my police report [no fee; it is free]. If applicable.
[OR]
To pay the fee for placing the freeze [look at this chart to determine if it is a fee:
http://www.transunion.com/sites/corporate/personal/fraudIdentityTheft/preventing/securityFreeze]
____ I have enclosed a personal check.

____ Please charge my credit card. It is a ____ (Visa, MasterCard, Discover, AmEx), the number is _____ and the expiration date is _____. My card identification number (three- or
four- digit number on back of card) is _____.
Sincerely,
[Signature]
Your name

Personal Info update Letter

Name
Address
Credit Bureau
Address
Date
Dear Credit Bureau,

This letter is a formal complaint that you are reporting inaccurate personal information. I am confused to see how many different variations of my name, address, employers and even my birth date is being reported. This is highly embarrassing to me and I am reporting to you the correct and legal versions of my personal information

I am reporting to you my correct personal information.
This is my correct personal information:
Name:

ADDRESS:
Employers:
Date of Birth:
01/01/1969
The following are incorrect and need to be deleted:
Names:
Addresses
123 This Street
River Rouge MI 48218
Employers:

Detroit Public Works
Date of Birth
01/01/1966
Telephone numbers:

THE TELEPHONE NUMBERS listed are old and no longer belong to me. I have no home phone, please delete these.

Spouse:
Name
I am not married; please remove the spouse's name Jimmy Cracked Corn. It should state none.

I am asking that you delete all the above incorrect information as it is incorrect. Please remove the above information as quickly as possible. I feel that it will be very harming to any future employers who might need to see my credit report. This report makes it seems as though I am twelve different people living in twelve different places, born at two different times.

I have enclosed copies of my current driver's license, light bill, and social security card as proof of my identity and my correct information.

Sincerely,
Name
SS
DOB
Enclosure

Multiple Inquiry Removal Letter

{Name}
{Address}
{Phone #}
{Credit Bureau: Name}
{Credit Bureau: Address}
{Date}
RE: Request for Investigation of Unauthorized Credit Inquiry
Dear Sir or Madam,

I checked my personal credit report, which I acquired from your organization on [insert date of report] and I noticed an unauthorized credit inquiry had been made.

I contacted [inquiry source's name], who conducted the inquiry and asked them to remove their credit inquiry from my credit profile.

I request that you initiate an investigation into [inquiry source's name] inquiry on my credit report to determine who authorized the inquiry. If, once your investigation is complete, you find my allegation to be true, please remove the inquiry and send me an updated copy of my credit report at the address listed above.

If you find the inquiry referenced above to be valid, please send me a description of the procedures used in your investigation within 15 business days of the completion of the investigation.

Thank you for your assistance in this matter,
{Signature}
{Printed Name}

BE SURE TO INCLUDE a copy of the credit report page evidencing the inquiry. It also does not hurt to highlight the section, just so there is no mistake. Otherwise, you run the risk of delaying the process and adding additional communication. Take the extra step ahead of time to save potential complications further down the road.

Medical HIPAA/Validation Request

Date:
Your Name
Your Address
Your City, State, Zip
Collection Agency Name
Collection Agency Address
Collection Agency City, State, Zip
RE: Account # (Fill in Account Number)
To Whom It May Concern:
Be advised this is not a refusal to pay, but a notice that your claim is disputed, and validation is requested. Under the Fair Debt collection Practices Act (FDCPA), I have the right to request validation of the debt you say I owe you. I am requesting proof that I am indeed the party you are asking to pay this debt, and there is some contractual obligation that is binding on me to pay this debt. This is NOT a request for "verification" or proof of my mailing address, but a request for VALIDATION made pursuant to 15 USC 1692g Sec. 809 (b) of the FDCPA. I respectfully request that your offices provide me with competent evidence that I have any legal obligation to pay you. At this time, I will also inform you that if your offices have or continue to report invalidated information to any of the three major credit bureaus (Equifax, Experian, Trans Union), this action might constitute fraud under both federal and state laws. Due to this fact if any negative mark is found or continues to report on any of my credit reports by your company or the company you represent, I will not hesitate in bringing legal action against you and your client for the following: Violation of the Fair Debt Collection

Practices Act and Defamation of Character.

I am sure your legal staff will agree that non-compliance with this request could put your company in serious legal trouble with the FTC and other state or federal agencies. If your offices can provide the proper documentation as requested in the following declaration, I will require 30 days to investigate this information and during such time all collection activity must cease and desist. Also, during this validation period if any action is taken which could be considered detrimental to any of my credit reports, I will consult with legal counsel for suit. This includes any listing of any information to a credit-reporting repository that could be inaccurate or invalidated. If your offices fail to respond to this validation request within 30 days from the date of your receipt, all references to this account must be deleted and completely removed from my credit file and a copy of such deletion request

shall be sent to me immediately.

It would be advisable that you and your client assure that your records are in order before I am forced to

take legal action.

CREDITOR/DEBT COLLECTOR DECLARATION

Please provide the following:

• Agreement with your client that grants you the authority to collect on this alleged debt.

• Agreement that bears the signature of the alleged debtor wherein he/she agreed to pay the creditor.

• Any insurance claims been made by any creditor regarding this account.

• Any Judgments obtained by any creditor regarding this account.

• Name and address of alleged creditor.

• Name on file of alleged debtor.

• Alleged account number.

• Address on file for alleged debtor.

• Amount of alleged debt.

- Date this alleged debt became payable.
- Date of original charge off or delinquency.
- Verification that this debt was assigned or sold to collector.
- Complete accounting of alleged debt.
- Commission for debt collector if collection efforts are successful.

Please provide the name and address of the bonding agent for «COLLECTIONAGENCY» in case legal action becomes necessary. Your claim cannot and WILL NOT be considered if any portion of the above is not completed and returned with copies of all requested documents. This is a request for validation made pursuant to the Fair Debt Collection Practices Act. Please allow 30 days for processing after I receive this information back.

Best Regards
[Your Signature]
cc Federal Trade Commission

Lexis Nexis Freeze Requests

D^{ate]}
LexisNexis Risk Solutions Consumer Center
P.O. Box 105108
Atlanta, GA 30348-5108
Dear LexisNexis:
I would like to place a security freeze on my LexisNexis credit file.
My full name is:
My current home address is:
My former address was:
My Social Security number is:
My date of birth is:
Yours truly,
[Your name and address]

OR PRINT THE PDF FROM LexisNexis website.
https://consumer.risk.lexisnexis.com/consumer

Repayment Agreement for Account

Creditor

Full, Legal Name of Payee
Full, Legal Name of Promisor
Loan Date
Total Amount of Loan
Final Due Date for Repayment
Agreement Terms:

I, Payee Name ("Payee"), borrowed $1,000 from Promisor Name ("Promisor") on Loan Date. By signing this agreement both Payee and Promisor acknowledge that Payee will pay back Promisor using the following payment schedule.

Payee agrees to repay Promisor with a personal check for $100 on the first of each month for 10 months beginning with January 1, 20__. The last payment will be made October 1, 20__, at which time the loan will be fully repaid.

Payee further agrees to pay a $35 per week late charge for every week that payment is delayed after the first of the month. This $35 late charge may be prorated as a $5 per day charge for each day that the payment is late for segments of time shorter than seven days.

Both Payee and Promisor agree to the payment agreement defined above.

Signed:

_____

Signature of Payee with Date

_____

Signature of Promisor with Date

_____

Signature of Witness or Notary with Date

Sample Debt Settlement Agreement Letter

Creditor

Name of Debtor
Address of Debtor
City, State, Zip Code
DATE
Name of Creditor
Address of Creditor
City, State, Zip Code
RE: Settlement of debt
Dear Name of Creditor:

This is a formal acknowledgement of our phone conversation on DATE in relation to settling my debt. We agreed that my outstanding debt is AMOUNT, and that you will accept the sum of LOWER AMOUNT.

We agreed that this will constitute payment in full and will discharge all due bills. Once the payment is made, no further steps will be taken on your part to collect the alleged debt. I will make the payment in full with a cashier's check within five days after this agreement is signed.

I understand that if the payment is not made according to the agreed time, this agreement is null and void and the full amount I owe will be due.

Once I have made the agreed payment, you will erase any negative information on my credit report and not place any negative information on my credit report in the future pertaining to this debt.

Please sign the included copy of this debt settlement agreement letter and return it to me. Thank you for your kind consideration in this matter. If you have any questions, I can be reached at Phone Number or Email Address.

Sincerely,

Signature of Debtor

Printed Name of Debtor

Signature of Creditor

Printed Name of Creditor

Request for Ceasing Phone Calls

Creditor

Date
Your Name
Address
City, State Zip
Debt Collector's Name
Address
City, State Zip
Re: Account Number
Dear Debt Collector:

Pursuant to my rights under federal debt collection laws, I am requesting that you cease and desist calling me, as well as my family and friends, in relation to this and all other alleged debts you claim I owe. Only communicate with me through mail.

You are hereby notified that if you do not comply with this request, I will immediately file a complaint with the Federal Trade Commission and the [your state here] Attorney General's office. Civil and criminal claims will be pursued.

Sincerely,
Your Name

609 Letters 1-4

Template #1
Name
Address
Phone Number
Account # (if available)
Name of Company/Point Person
Relevant Department
Address
Date
Dear [Name of credit reporting agency],

I am writing to exercise my right to question the validity of the debt your agency claims I owe, pursuant to the Fair Credit Reporting Act (FCRA).

As stated in Section 609 of the FCRA, (2) (E): A consumer reporting agency is not required to remove accurate derogatory information from a consumer's file unless the information is outdated under Section 609 or cannot be verified.

As is my right, I am requesting verification of the following items:

[List any/all items you are looking to dispute, including the account name(s) and number(s) as listed on your credit report]

Additionally, I have highlighted these items on the attached copy of the credit report I received.

I request that all future correspondence be done through the mail or email. As stated in the FCRA, you are required to respond to my dispute within 30 days of receipt of this letter. If you fail to offer a response, all disputed information must be deleted.

Thank you for your prompt attention to this matter.

Sincerely
[Your signature]
[Your name]
See Attached: [List attached documents here.]
[*Attach copies of proof of identity (name, birth date, SSN, current mailing address) along with a copy of your credit report with relevant items highlighted, as discussed above: "What to Include in Your Dispute."]
Template #2
Name
Address
Phone Number
Account # (if available)
Name of Company/Point Person
Relevant Department
Address
Date
Dear Sir or Madam,

I am writing to exercise my right to dispute the following items on my file. I have made note of these items on the attached copy of the report I have received from your agency. You will also find attached copies of documents that prove my identity, birth date, SSN, and address.

As is stated in the Fair Credit Reporting Act (FCRA), Section 609:
[In this section, include a relevant quote based on which area you are trying to dispute. Several quotes are See Attached: [List attached documentation here.]
listed above, or you can look on the FTC's website for the official document with exact verbiage. Make sure you note which sub-section you are quoting from.]

The items I wish to dispute are as follows:

[Include as many relevant items as you have, up to 20, including the account name and number as listed on your credit report.]

These are [incorrect, inaccurate, unverified] due to the lack of validation by numerous parties that is required by Section 609. I have attached copies of relevant documentation.

I would appreciate your assistance in investigating this matter within the next 30 days. As required by the FCRA, if you fail to do so, all information/disputed items must be deleted from the report.

Sincerely,
[Your signature]
[Your name]
See attached: [List attached documentation here.]
Template #3
Name
Address
Phone Number
Account # (if available)
Name of Company/Point Person
Relevant Department
Address
To whom it may concern,

This letter is a formal dispute in accordance with the Fair Credit Reporting Act (FCRA).

Upon review of my credit report, I have found that there are several inaccurate and unverified items. These have negatively impacted my ability to receive credit and have provided unnecessary embarrassment and inconvenience.

As I am sure you are aware, it is my right, according to Section 609 of the FCRA, to request a proper investigation into these inaccuracies. In particular, I am referencing Section 609 (c) (B) (iii), which lists "the right of a consumer to dispute information in the file of the consumer" under the "model summary of the rights of consumers."

As such, the following are items I wish to dispute on my credit report:

[Include as many relevant items as you have, up to 20, including each account name and number as listed on your report.]

I have also highlighted all relevant items on the attached copy of said credit report.

As stated in the FCRA, you are required to respond to my dispute within 30 days of receipt of this letter. If you fail to offer a response, all disputed information must be deleted. I have attached all relevant documentation for your review. I thank you in advance for your prompt response and resolution of this issue.

Sincerely,

[Your signature]

[Your name]

See Attached: [List each piece of attached documentation here.]

Template #4: Follow-up Letter

Name

Address

Phone Number

Account # (if available)

Name of Company/Point Person

Relevant Department

Address

Date

Dear Sir or Madam,

My name is [Your name], and I reached out to you several weeks ago regarding my credit report. This letter is to notify you that you have not responded to my initial letter, dated [insert date]. I have restated the terms of my dispute below for your convenience.

[Insert information from your first letter about disputed items. Include disputed account names and numbers as listed on your credit report.]

Section 609 of the Fair Credit Reporting Act (FCRA) states that you must investigate my dispute within 30 calendar days from my initial letter. As you have failed to do so, I kindly request that you remove the aforementioned items from my credit report.

Any further comments or questions can be directed to my legal representative, [insert name], who can be reached at [insert phone number].

Sincerely,

[Your signature]

[Your name]

See Attached: [List all attached documentation here, including copies of your credit report, proof of identity, proof of current mailing address, etc.]

www.ingramcontent.com/pod-product-compliance
Lightning Source LLC
Chambersburg PA
CBHW060901170526
45158CB00001B/441